OPPOSING
VIEWPOINTS®
SERIES

| The Culture of Beauty

Other Books of Related Interest

Opposing Viewpoints Series

Eating Disorders
Feminism
The Fashion Industry

At Issue Series

How Does Advertising Impact Teen Behavior?
Beauty Pageants
Body Piercing and Tattoos

Current Controversies Series

The Elderly

"Congress shall make
no law … abridging
the freedom of speech,
or of the press."

First Amendment to the US Constitution

The basic foundation of our democracy is the First Amendment guarantee of freedom of expression. The Opposing Viewpoints Series is dedicated to the concept of this basic freedom and the idea that it is more important to practice it than to enshrine it.

The Culture of Beauty

Louise I. Gerdes, Book Editor

GREENHAVEN PRESS
A part of Gale, Cengage Learning

Detroit • New York • San Francisco • New Haven, Conn • Waterville, Maine • London

Elizabeth Des Chenes, *Director, Publishing Solutions*

© 2013 Greenhaven Press, a part of Gale, Cengage Learning

Gale and Greenhaven Press are registered trademarks used herein under license.

For more information, contact:
Greenhaven Press
27500 Drake Rd.
Farmington Hills, MI 48331-3535
Or you can visit our Internet site at gale.cengage.com.

For product information and technology assistance, contact us at:

Gale Customer Support, 1-800-877-4253.
For permission to use material from this text or product, submit all requests online at www.cengage.com/permissions.

Further permissions questions can be emailed to permissionrequest@cengage.com.

Articles in Greenhaven Press anthologies are often edited for length to meet page requirements. In addition, original titles of these works are changed to clearly present the main thesis and to explicitly indicate the author's opinion. Every effort is made to ensure that Greenhaven Press accurately reflects the original intent of the authors. Every effort has been made to trace the owners of copyrighted material.

Cover image © Nuzza/Shutterstock.com.

LIBRARY OF CONGRESS CATALOGING-IN-PUBLICATION DATA

The culture of beauty / Louise I. Gerdes, book editor.
    p. cm. -- (Opposing viewpoints)
    Includes bibliographical references and index.
    ISBN 978-0-7377-6310-2 (hardcover) -- ISBN 978-0-7377-6311-9 (pbk.)
1. Feminine beauty (Aesthetics) 2. Beauty, Personal--Psychological aspects.
3. Body image. 4. Aesthetics--Social aspects. I. Gerdes, Louise I., 1953-
    HQ1219.C832 2013
    646.7'042--dc23

                             2012043097

Printed in the United States of America
1 2 3 4 5 6 7 17 16 15 14 13

Contents

Why Consider Opposing Viewpoints?

> "The only way in which a human being
> can make some approach to knowing
> the whole of a subject is by hearing
> what can be said about it by persons of
> every variety of opinion and studying
> all modes in which it can be looked at
> by every character of mind. No wise
> man ever acquired his wisdom in any
> mode but this."
>
> *John Stuart Mill*

In our media-intensive culture it is not difficult to find differing opinions. Thousands of newspapers and magazines and dozens of radio and television talk shows resound with differing points of view. The difficulty lies in deciding which opinion to agree with and which "experts" seem the most credible. The more inundated we become with differing opinions and claims, the more essential it is to hone critical reading and thinking skills to evaluate these ideas. Opposing Viewpoints books address this problem directly by presenting stimulating debates that can be used to enhance and teach these skills. The varied opinions contained in each book examine many different aspects of a single issue. While examining these conveniently edited opposing views, readers can develop critical thinking skills such as the ability to compare and contrast authors' credibility, facts, argumentation styles, use of persuasive techniques, and other stylistic tools. In short, the Opposing Viewpoints Series is an ideal way to attain the higher-level thinking and reading skills so essential in a culture of diverse and contradictory opinions.

In addition to providing a tool for critical thinking, Opposing Viewpoints books challenge readers to question their own strongly held opinions and assumptions. Most people form their opinions on the basis of upbringing, peer pressure, and personal, cultural, or professional bias. By reading carefully balanced opposing views, readers must directly confront new ideas as well as the opinions of those with whom they disagree. This is not to argue simplistically that everyone who reads opposing views will—or should—change his or her opinion. Instead, the series enhances readers' understanding of their own views by encouraging confrontation with opposing ideas. Careful examination of others' views can lead to the readers' understanding of the logical inconsistencies in their own opinions, perspective on why they hold an opinion, and the consideration of the possibility that their opinion requires further evaluation.

Evaluating Other Opinions

To ensure that this type of examination occurs, Opposing Viewpoints books present all types of opinions. Prominent spokespeople on different sides of each issue as well as well-known professionals from many disciplines challenge the reader. An additional goal of the series is to provide a forum for other, less known, or even unpopular viewpoints. The opinion of an ordinary person who has had to make the decision to cut off life support from a terminally ill relative, for example, may be just as valuable and provide just as much insight as a medical ethicist's professional opinion. The editors have two additional purposes in including these less known views. One, the editors encourage readers to respect others' opinions—even when not enhanced by professional credibility. It is only by reading or listening to and objectively evaluating others' ideas that one can determine whether they are worthy of consideration. Two, the inclusion of such viewpoints encourages the important critical thinking skill of objectively evaluating an author's credentials and bias. This evaluation will illuminate an author's reasons for taking a particular stance on an issue and will aid in readers' evaluation of the author's ideas.

It is our hope that these books will give readers a deeper understanding of the issues debated and an appreciation of the complexity of even seemingly simple issues when good and honest people disagree. This awareness is particularly important in a democratic society such as ours in which people enter into public debate to determine the common good. Those with whom one disagrees should not be regarded as enemies but rather as people whose views deserve careful examination and may shed light on one's own.

Thomas Jefferson once said that "difference of opinion leads to inquiry, and inquiry to truth." Jefferson, a broadly educated man, argued that "if a nation expects to be ignorant and free . . . it expects what never was and never will be." As individuals and as a nation, it is imperative that we consider the opinions of others and examine them with skill and discernment. The Opposing Viewpoints Series is intended to help readers achieve this goal.

David L. Bender and Bruno Leone,
Founders

Introduction

"Since the 1980s, the Cinderella story and other similar 'transformation narratives' are increasingly being woven though popular culture: consumer advertising, media images, and television shows . . . illustrate for many mainstream American women Cinderella-like transformations."

Julie M. Albright, professor of . sociology, University of Southern California.

The importance of beauty as a personal trait, particularly for girls and women, is repeated throughout childhood in stories and books, on television, and in movies. Indeed, in children's stories such as "Cinderella," "Snow White," and "Sleeping Beauty," the value of female beauty is one of the primary themes. For example, unlike her "ugly" stepsisters, Cinderella is both "good" and beautiful beneath all that soot. Once the cinders are removed from her face, Cinderella is transformed into a great beauty and as a result marries the prince and lives happily ever after. This story reinforces what studies often show: that attractive people are perceived to be good and trustworthy like Cinderella, while less than attractive people are seen as bad and underhanded like Cinderella's stepsisters. The Cinderella story also reinforces the message that physical beauty is a way of escaping a life of desperation and hard work. Indeed, studies show that attractive people do make more money. Like Cinderella, beautiful women are also often chosen as mates by economically successful men. As author Sheila Jeffreys asserts, "women want to be chosen, and men are programmed to choose beautiful women."[1] Thus in the eyes of many, to be beautiful is a significant asset.

Since the beauty that girls often see portrayed in these childhood stories, in their dolls, in magazine images, on television, and in movies does not come naturally for most, beauty must be something to work toward—what some commentators call the body as a project. Self-improvement is not new, but the goal of self-improvement has changed in recent decades. In her book, *The Body Project: An Intimate History of American Girls*, Joan Brumberg compared the diaries of young girls in the 1800s with those of the late 1990s. In the 1800s, girls were more concerned about "good works," such as charitable activities and the performance of good deeds. Unlike girls of the late 1990s, girls during the 1800s rarely mentioned efforts to improve their bodies or faces. Today, on the other hand, girls are more interested in "good looks"—the pursuit of beauty. As a result, companies that sell cosmetics, personal care products, exercise programs, and diet pills earn billions of dollars each year. Fashion and style magazines further emphasize the importance of the body project in both editorial content and advertising by setting the standards of beauty to which many girls and women aspire. While few would dispute that self-improvement is admirable, some are concerned with studies that show an increasing number of girls and women who are dissatisfied with their bodies, a rise in eating disorders, and a general increase in the acceptance of cosmetic surgery—the ultimate body project. Analysts offer a variety of explanations for the change in attitudes that are reflected in the controversies concerning the culture of beauty.

One explanation for the late-twentieth-century interest in the pursuit of beauty comes from feminist writers. Some feminist analysts assert that male institutions keep women focused on achieving increasingly unrealistic standards of beauty as a response to their rise in power. In her 1991 book *The Beauty Myth*, Naomi Wolf asserts that as the number of women pursuing careers and political influence began to rise during the 1970s and 1980s, the myth that women should aspire to near impossible standards of beauty was necessary to supplant the myths devised to control previous generations of women—the myths of motherhood, domesticity, chastity, and passivity. In Wolf's view, "the gaunt, youthful model [has] supplanted the happy housewife as the arbiter of successful womanhood."[2] Reflecting on her book twenty years later, Wolf explains that when the book was published, she "noted a burgeoning epidemic of eating disorders was engulfing what should have been the feistiest, most confident generation of women ever. The field of cosmetic surgery, especially breast implant procedures, was booming [and] . . . insult-ridden advertisements for anti-aging creams were shaping the way women thought about the experience of getting older. The way we looked determined our value to society." Sadly, she notes, these concerns have actually increased. "The body size of fashion models and starlets has dropped still further; fashion ads showcase women who look as if they should be hospitalized. The technologies of cosmetic surgery have become so commonplace that there are communities in which women with unreconstructed faces are seen as bucking the norm," she asserts. Nevertheless, Wolf claims, she was surprised by a changing social norm surrounding aging. For example, she notes that "there is now an influential and growing demographic of educated, well-off women whose status, sense of self-esteem and sexual cachet rise rather than fall as they head toward midlife. I do not see younger women looking at accomplished women in their 40s with pity or derision: I see them looking ahead with admiration and even envy."[3]

Another explanation for the shift from self-improvement through good works to the pursuit of beauty is the emergence of a consumer society in which the market constantly creates new needs and desires and in turn new products to meet those needs and desires. According to sociologist Julie M. Albright, "The body has increasingly become [the market's] terrain over the years, and larger and larger segments of women's and girls' bodies have become colonized, commodified, and reshaped by market forces."[4] As a result, these commentators claim, the beauty industry has grown from $40 million in sales in 1914 to about $20 billion a year today. To enhance sales of beauty products, advertisers constantly raise the beauty bar by using unnaturally thin models and digital photo altering techniques, the critics maintain. According to Brumberg, "Commercial interests play directly to the body angst of young girls, a marketing strategy that results in enormous revenues for manufacturers of skin and hair products as well as diet foods."[5] The strategy is working, these analysts assert, as studies link body dissatisfaction and the desire to be thin with the consumption of fashion magazines and television.

The success of this strategy has also had a global impact. In an international study sponsored by the Dove Campaign for Real Beauty of thirty-two hundred women worldwide found that only 2 percent of women from ten countries consider themselves "beautiful." Indeed, the study found that 60 percent of these women agreed that "society expects women to enhance their appearance."[6]

Still another explanation for the shift from internal to external self-improvement is the growing media emphasis on celebrity culture. According to New York plastic surgeon Z. Paul Lorenc, one of several concerns is that more and more Americans are seeking plastic surgery because of the very high beauty bar set by celebrities. He is concerned not so much with the extremes such as those who participate in the MTV reality show *I Want a Famous Face* but with those hoping to capture the youth and glamour associated with celebrities. He claims that celebrity culture perpetuates a worship of youthfulness. According to Lorenc, even celebrities are not exempt. "They have an image they have to upkeep and are forced to do that with Botox. They have to maintain an image and a lifestyle and an income."[7] Indeed, "plastic-surgery watching" is a popular pastime in magazines and on celebrity-watching websites. If the celebrities themselves are not altered with surgery, some of their images are altered with digital technologies such as Photoshop. Actress Kate Winslet claims that her legs had been digitally reduced by 30 percent on a *GQ* magazine cover. She told ABC News in 2009, "I did realise a few years ago that no one actually talks about this retouching thing. It's like a secret or something. I'm damned if it's going to be a secret any more. I really want these young women to know we don't look like this."[8]

While the source of the shift from the pursuit of "good works" to the pursuit of "good looks" remains subject to debate, most agree that the number of girls and women who are dissatisfied with their bodies, the increase in the number of people diagnosed with eating disorders, and the normalization of cosmetic surgery poses a problem for the mental health of women and girls and, increasingly, for boys and men, as well. How best to balance public health with economic freedom and free expression remains hotly contested as the viewpoints in the following chapters reveal. The authors of the viewpoints in *Opposing Viewpoints: Culture of Beauty* explore these and other issues in the following chapters: How Are Standards of Beauty Established?, What Impacts Do Ideals of Beauty Have on Society?, Should People Strive for Beauty?, What Are the Societal Effects of the Beauty and Fashion Industries? Whether patriarchal institutions, a consumer society, or celebrity culture are responsible for the need to pursue increasingly higher standards of beauty, some—even *The Beauty Myth* author, Naomi Wolf—are optimistic that attitudes are changing. She suggests, "Today, the notion that beauty ideals are socially constructed, manipulated by advertisers, and marked for profit motives is part of the conventional wisdom, not a fringe argument. Smart advertisers for beauty products court women's raised confidence." Indeed, she concludes, "the archetype of the Evil Queen and Sleeping Beauty has been laid to rest."[9]

Notes

1. Sheila Jeffreys, *Beauty and Misogyny*. London: Routledge, 2005.
2. Naomi Wolf, *The Beauty Myth*. New York: William Morrow, 1991.

3. Naomi Wolf, "A Wrinkle in Time," *Washington Post*, May 27, 2011.
4. Julie M. Albright, "Impossible Bodies," *Configurations*, Spring 2007.
5. Joan Brumberg, *The Body Project: An Intimate History of Americans Girls*. New York: Random House, 1978.
6. StrategyOne, *The Real Truth About Beauty: A Global Report*, 2004.
7. Z. Paul Lorenc and Trisha Hall, *A Little Work: Behind the Doors of a Park Avenue Plastic Surgeon*. New York: St. Martin's, 2004.
8. Quoted in Brooke Eaton, "Kate Winslet Says You Don't Have to Be a Size 2," June 4, 2012. http://magazine.foxnews.com.
9. Wolf, "A Wrinkle in Time."

CHAPTER 1

How Are Standards of Beauty Established?

Chapter Preface

One of the controversies in the debate concerning how standards of beauty are established is whether the beauty industry itself can change beauty standards that some believe threaten the emotional, physical, and psychological health of women and girls. In 2004, Dove—a personal care products company and subsidiary of Unilever, a British-Dutch multinational consumer goods company—launched its Campaign for Real Beauty. The goal of the campaign was to encourage women to celebrate natural physical variations among themselves and to inspire women and girls to be confident and comfortable with themselves. The campaign included billboards and advertisements that pictured amateur models of varying body types and sizes posing in underwear. The campaign also distributed the video *Evolution*, in which time-lapsed photography shows how a plain girl is turned into a glamorous model with make-up and photographic techniques. The film then shows how the beauty of the model is further enhanced when the photographs are edited with Photoshop, an image-altering computer program. The film ends with the words, "No wonder our perception of beauty is distorted."[1] In the short film *Onslaught*, a little girl is bombarded with videos, product shots, and ads illustrating impossible beauty standards. The short film ends with the same girl walking to school and the words, "Talk to your daughter before the beauty industry does."[2] Although the films won awards, and Dove has been lauded for its efforts, some claim that fashion industry images are not meant to reflect the average woman, while others question whether shifting the responsibility for countering the barrage of unrealistic media images to parents is fair.

Washington Post staff writer Robin Givhan maintains that fashion models are professionals who are paid to be thin and beautiful. She compares models to professional athletes who are "paid to maintain a fighting weight and breathtaking physique.

Yet no one complains that championship marathoners, tennis stars and volleyball players, with their impossibly taut bodies, dominate the covers of sports magazines, posing a threat to the delicate psyche of weekend athletes everywhere." In her view, the goal of fashion is to create fantasy images for readers. While she agrees that to occasionally remind readers that fashion is not reality is healthy, she challenges the value of Dove's amateur underwear models appearing on buses and billboards, reasoning that "no one wants to feel as though they've stumbled into the ladies' locker room or caught their neighbors in their skivvies."[3]

Other commentators challenge the campaign's claim that parents alone should be responsible for counteracting the flood of images and other social forces that threaten the self-esteem of their daughters. Harvard University law professor Jon D. Hanson argues that asking parents, in short films such as *Onslaught*, to battle the barrage of unrealistic images with which the beauty industry assaults their children "is equivalent to telling parents to teach their children how to float in thin air before gravity gets to them." Not only do children see these images, but their friends and their families—indeed all of society sees these images so that the standards they portray have become cultural expectations. Moreover, Hanson reasons, "If the industry is the problem, it strikes me as odd that the parents are supposed to be the solution." Hanson reveals that Dove is not a friend, nor a person, nor even a company. Dove is a brand, and its own parent company is one of the worst offenders, selling other personal care products using unrealistic beauty images. Indeed, he concludes, Unilever is doing nothing to stem its own standards of beauty "onslaught."[4]

Whether the beauty industry can or should be responsible for changing the standards of beauty or stemming the barrage of images that perpetuate these standards remains controversial. The authors in the following chapter present their views in other controversies surrounding the question, how are standards of beauty established? Whether the fashion and beauty industry will establish more accepting standards of beauty remains to be seen. *Culture Magazine* writer Hannah McGregor is cautiously optimistic: "Maybe one day the voice telling us it's okay to have a big butt won't also be telling us to hurry out and buy something to take care of that unsightly cellulite."[5]

Notes

1. *Evolution*, directed by Yael Staav and Tim Piper, October 6, 2006. www.youtube.com/watch?v=hibyAJOSW8U.
2. *Onslaught*, directed by Tim Piper, October 1, 2007. www.youtube.com/watch?v=Ei6JvK0W60I.
3. Robin Givhan, "Sorry, Dove: Bigger Isn't Necessarily Better," *Washington Post*, August 19, 2005.
4. Jon Hanson, "Hey Dove! Talk to YOUR Parent!," *Situationist*, September 21, 2009.
5. Hannah McGregor, "Dove Real Beauty Campaign: Can the Beauty Industry Scrap Its Own Standards of Beauty?," *Culture Magazine*, December 31, 2007.

> "*Standards of beauty cannot be just cultural artefacts. Biological factors (evolved instincts) must be at play.*"

Standards of Beauty Are Determined by Evolutionary Biology

Glenn Wilson

According to the theory of evolutionary biology, beauty standards are those characteristics that will attract a mate who will pass genes on to the next generation, claims psychology professor Glenn Wilson in the following viewpoint. For example, facial qualities such as symmetry and sexual dimorphism—traits that are clearly male or female—signal reproductive fitness, he asserts. Evolutionary biology also determines standards of body beauty, Wilson argues, as men prefer women with a much narrower waist than hips, an indicator of high levels of female hormones. However, he suggests, culture does account for some variations in beauty standards that relate to social aspects of mate quality, such as wealth. Wilson is a pioneer in evolutionary theories of sex differences, attraction, and love.

As you read, consider the following questions:

1. According to Wilson, what is the first principle of beauty that determines the attractiveness of the female face?
2. What influences a a woman's preference for a man who is macho versus one who is baby-faced, in the author's view?
3. In the author's opinion, how does human behavior in a nightclub reflect principles of evolutionary biology?

According to [filmmaker] Woody Allen, "only two things in life are important: one is sex, and the other isn't all that important". This is a view that is pretty much shared by evolutionary psychologists, who argue that the key motive is the 'sexual imperative', the need to pass our genes on to the following generation. Genes that do not succeed in reproducing themselves are lost forever. Everything else, including our survival instinct, is subservient to this central aim.

The essential first step is to attract a mate, preferably several to choose among. However, choice is more relevant to women than to men, who can potentially breed with several women in parallel. . . .

The first principle of beauty, though 'generalisation' might be a better word, is that female faces are seen as attractive when they *borrow baby signals*. Among these are smooth, pinkish skin, large open eyes, full lips and a small chin. These traits have apparently been evolved to evoke parental protection from men. Pop songs refer to adult women as 'baby', while pornographers call them 'babes'. Pets use similar infant signals to evoke caretaking in humans. (It is even possible that the tendency for men to go bald as they get older is an appeal to the maternal instinct of their wives after their masculine appeal is no longer credible.) The evolutionary reason for women's adoption of baby-doll features is that women are more fertile, and therefore more valued, when young. The breeding potential of men is less dependent on their age. Toyboys do exist (ask Mrs. Robinson[1]) but are rarer and seldom lasting.

Facial Beauty Cues

As a general rule, facial beauty depends on signals of *reproductive fitness*. In other words, both men and women look for markers of fertility and good parent potential. Primary among such cues are:

Averageness. Since the classic demonstrations of [anthropologist] Sir Francis Galton, it has been recognised that when photos of several faces are superimposed one on another, the composites appear as attractive. This is partly because blemishes and abnormalities are cancelled and the skin appears smooth, hence healthy. Average faces may also signal heterogeneity (outbreeding) which has advantages in breadth of immunity.

Symmetry. When the left and right sides are blended, a face is judged more attractive and having more 'mate appeal'. Symmetry implies 'developmental stability', which refers to a history of resistance to stresses during development, such as mutations, parasites and toxins. This principle applies equally to women and men. There is evidence that the partners of symmetrical men have more orgasms, presumably because such men are more desirable.

Sexual dimorphism. Feminine faces are attractive to men and exaggerations of femininity even more so. While average female faces are attractive, optimal attractiveness has slightly different proportions. These are the hyperfemale traits that are typically emphasised by make-up (bigger eyes, narrower eyebrows, pinker complexion, fuller redder lips, etc.). These are usually the attributes of young, mature women of around 24 years old, although some are younger still (e.g., the ideal lips are those typical of a 14 year girl). Not surprisingly, the composites of female models are more attractive than those based on randomly chosen women. Since these traits are estrogen markers, composites of women high in estrogen are judged by men as more desirable than those of women low in estrogen.

The Preferences of Women

Women are, of course, more complicated in their preferences. Sometimes they like manly, dominant (high testosterone) faces; at other times they prefer a softer look. [Researchers D.I.] Perrett, et al., found that women often prefer a slightly feminised male face (smaller chin, wider lips, larger eyes and higher arched eyebrows), no doubt because these suggest traits like empathy and reliability that might make for good parenting. Interestingly, the fossil record suggests that sexual dimorphism in humans has diminished over the last 100,000 years, presumably as a result of a female preference for caring men.

Whether a woman prefers a man who is macho or baby-faced, genetically similar or not, depends upon whether she is in *long-term or short-term mating mode*. There is a shift toward a preference for 'real' men, and those less closely related, when a woman is in mid-cycle, not pregnant, not on the contraceptive pill and when she is engaged in extra-pair mating (having an affair). In other words, when *fertile* women seek 'good genes', otherwise they favour 'resource provision'. Use of the pill removes the mid-cycle change in mate preference.

A similar principle applies to reactions to *dilated eye pupils*. Dilated pupils are generally attractive because they make the eyes look bigger and give the impression that the other person is interested in us. This helps to make a candle-lit dinner romantic—pupils are initially enlarged because the light is dim, but this is instinctively read by the partner across the table as emotional arousal, thus setting up a spiral of mutual desire.

Where men are concerned, the larger a woman's pupils the better. For women, large pupils are only preferred when they are mid-cycle, not on the pill, and are the type [that] likes 'bad boys' (all indicative of a short-term mating mode). When a long-term mate is sought, women prefer medium pupils because the male partner is seen as a better potential parent.

Which is more important in determining physical attractiveness, the body or the face? [T.E.] Currie and [A.C.] Little had models rated separately for body and face, then the two combined. Overall, the face was the better predictor of overall attractiveness. However, the body component increased in importance when men were considering women for short-term affairs as against a long-term relationship. No such shift occurred when women evaluated men. It is thus not surprising that women regard wandering eyes as a bad sign in a man.

Males seem to be more excited by female beauty than vice versa. [J.] Cloutier, et al., found that brain reward circuits in the *nucleus accumbens* and *orbitofrontal cortex* [OFC] showed greater fMRI [functional magnetic resonance imaging] activation (signal change relative to baseline) when people viewed attractive faces relative to unattractive faces. However, males responded more differentially (especially in the OFC, where females did not distinguish at all). This confirms the widespread idea that, where sexual matters are concerned, men are more visual animals than women. However, women differentiate more than men in the smell channel.

Beauty vs. Sex Appeal

Sex appeal is not the same as beauty and is perhaps more complex. . . .

By and large, sex appeal derives from the typical differences between men and women, for example, the female hourglass figure versus the V-shaped torso of men, the greater height and depth of voice of men, and the 'musky' smell of men versus the 'sweet' smell of women. These are markers of *sex hormones* (especially estrogen versus testosterone) and they signal reproductive fitness.

For women, a key marker of fertility is the *waist/hip ratio*. Low ratios, with the waist much narrower than the hips (ideally .7 to .8) are attractive to men because they indicate high estrogen. By corollary, a tight, compact backside in a man is preferred by women. Strangely, women even seem to prefer it in themselves, being famously concerned about whether 'their bum looks big'

Theories of Beauty

Pythagoras put forward a theory that physical beauty derived from the subject's proportions and the golden ratio in the sixth century BC, and fields as diverse as art, sociology, and cosmetic surgery have also addressed the subject. However, the evolutionary psychological approach is unique, in that it proposes a scientific basis couched in evolutionary logic for why we perceive certain markers to be more attractive than others. Its practitioners argue that the features that men and women find attractive are biological signals of a good-quality mate.

Thomas Gizbert, TTHblog, *September 28, 2011. http://triplehelixblog.com.*

in whatever they are wearing. Perhaps they would be more reassured by reading some evolutionary psychology than soliciting their partner's opinion.

Innate Visual Templates Influence Survival

Ethologists (scientists who study animal instincts) have shown that all species are equipped with certain *innate releasing mechanisms* [IRM]—stimulus patterns that are primed through evolution to evoke behaviour of survival importance. For example, humans readily acquire a fear of snakes and spiders because they were particularly dangerous to our ancestors, whereas we don't fear cars half as much as we should.

The human male seems to have an innate tendency to be turned on by paired, pink, fleshy hemispheres. Desmond Morris has argued that breasts excite men because they 'echo' the rear presentation signal that is a key IRM for the human male. Support for such an idea comes from observation of certain primates, such as the gelada baboon, in which the female has copied her rear configuration onto her front side for purposes both of sexual titillation and appeasement.

Such innate visual templates are subject to modification and consolidation in early childhood in accord with what is actually experienced in the environment. This is called *imprinting*, and it accounts for some cultural variability as well as attachments to inappropriate targets that we dub *fetishism*. Fetish objects are not determined by random conditioning; they nearly always have a strong sensory or symbolic association with the innate releaser. For example, a black high-heeled shoe is roughly the shape, colour and size of the pubic triangle; it traps pheromones after being worn, and has dominant, adult female (superbitch) connotations. Not surprisingly, shoe fetishists are more common than lawn-mower fetishists. Shoe fetishists are also more common than hat fetishists, which perhaps connects with the fact that shoes are more prominent in the sightline of a crawling infant than hats (infancy being the time when fetishisms are established.)

Attracting Mates Through Display

Both men and women *display* in order to attract mates. Nightclubs operate as human *leks* (sexual display grounds). Observations of people going in and out of nightclubs show that 50% more people leave as couples than arrive together. Males approach females in accordance with the tightness of their clothes, the amount of flesh they expose (especially in the breast area) and the provocativeness of their dancing. These, in turn, vary with the phase of their cycle. When fertile, women wear sexier clothes, display more flesh and dance more provocatively. The most successful females display at least 40% of their body and 50% of their breast area. The limit of exposure is apparently the point where 'allure' becomes 'brazenness' (signalling promiscuity and possibly inviting rape). Women choose among the males brave (dominant) enough to ask them to dance.

Male displays are more focused on demonstrations of power and achievement (c.f., the colourful constructions of the New Guinea bower bird). A man shown seated in a Bentley Continental is rated as more attractive by women than the same man in a Ford Fiesta, whereas men are little influenced by such status manipulation in their judgements of women. However, men do seem to recognise when they are impressing women—their testosterone increases after driving a Porsche in public and decreases after driving a banger [clunker].

Clearly, *wealth and status* are more important markers of 'mate value' to women than physical good looks. In fact, body builders are likely to be seen by women as self-absorbed narcissists. Intelligence, creativity, sense of humour and generosity (willingness to share resources) are, however, highly rated by women.

It is widely supposed that eligibility in a man depends on his availability. But this is another respect in which women are complicated. Single women complain that 'all the good men are taken' but the truth seems to be that being already taken makes a man more attractive. [J.] Parker and [M.] Burkley found that single women were more attracted to a man if they thought he was already attached. No such 'mate poaching' preference was observed for either men (who pursue female targets indiscriminately) or attached women (who prefer single targets).

There is much consistency across cultures as to who is attractive. The principles of averageness, symmetry, sexual dimorphism and familiarity apply equally in non-Western cultures. Infants (2–3 months old) share the same standards of beauty as adults, preferring to look at faces that adults find attractive, so standards of beauty cannot be just cultural artefacts. Biological factors (evolved instincts) must be at play, and as we have noted, these universal preferences derive from signals of *mate quality* (indications of youth, health, fitness and fertility).

Accounting for Variations

Some variations across time and place do need accounting for. Generally, they relate to more social aspects of mate quality (signals of wealth and status). For example, the value of a suntan has varied throughout history. Pale skin was sought in Elizabethan days because exposure to the sun implied peasant status. Since the industrial revolution, a suntan became valued because workers were confined to mines and factories, while the rich could afford foreign holidays. Thinness (to the point of anorexia) is prized in Western society, though by women more than men. Models appearing in women's magazines are thinner than those that adorn the pages of men's magazines. Fatness of the kind associated with Turkish belly dancers may be valued where food privation means that only the rich can get fat. Youth is prized in Western society; less so in tribal cultures that venerate elders, where pendulous breasts may be preferred over those that are pert.

We tend to value traits that are typical within our own group—hairiness in Scots, smoothness in Chinese, large breasts in Hollywood and the protruding buttocks of Hottentot women. This could be the origins of racial and species divergence and it raises another explanation as to why average faces are attractive. According to *prototype theory*, we are most comfortable with patterns we have come to expect, since these are easier to process in the brain. [P.] Winkielman, et al., demonstrated this *exposure principle* with abstract stimuli (patterns of dots) but believed it would generalise to human beauty.

Familiarity is a learning mechanism that could help to explain *genetic similarity attraction* (the tendency to prefer those closely related to and resembling ourselves) as well as *idolisation* (obsession with celebrities, even those that are totally empty).

No doubt avatars of beauty are affected by experience and media repetition though that is not the whole story.

An interesting historic variation in standards of beauty is described by [T.] Pettijohn and [B.J.] Jungeberg. They found that men's perception of sex appeal depends upon a nation's *economic health*. Playboy models tended to be more big-eyed, petite and feminine during good times; more mature and motherly in times of economic difficulty. Apparently, we seek fun when things are going well and support/security when times are bad. . . .

The Driving Factors of Our Evolution

Human evolution is driven by sexual selection as much as by natural selection.

What we are today is partly the result of the sexual preferences of our ancestors.

Beauty and sex appeal are not inherent in stimulus patterns but rooted in our responses. They are based primarily on signals of health, reproductive and parental fitness, although familiarity may also contribute. We are seldom conscious of the adaptive value of our choices but simply go on 'instinct'.

Finally, we should not make the mistake of assuming the opposite gender thinks like ourselves. Men and women differ in the field of mating and dating perhaps more than any other. There is much truth in the adage that 'men are only after one thing, whereas women are after *everything*'.

Note

1. Mrs. Robinson, a middle-aged character in the 1967 movie *The Graduate*, seduces the main character—a younger man and recent college graduate who then falls in love with her daughter.

> "The concept of the ideal body is a
> cultural construct, . . . [but] facial
> beauty is a biologically ingrained
> concept."

Facial Beauty Standards Are Universal While Body Beauty Standards Are Cultural

Michal Brichacek and Robert Moreland

Although cultural factors influence what men consider an attractive female body, facial beauty is universal, assert University of Western Ontario medical students Michal Brichacek and Robert Moreland in the following viewpoint. They cite, for example, studies in which Japanese men prefer images of women with less body fat than the women whom Britons prefer. Studies of facial beauty, however, reveal that people from all cultures prefer facial symmetry and "average" faces without particularly unique features, claim Brichacek and Moreland. Although the impact of Western media may influence studies of body beauty, studies of faces show that facial traits transcend cultural and media influences, the authors maintain.

Michal Brichacek and Robert Moreland, "Is Beauty Truly in the Eye of the Beholder?: The Universal Nature of Facial Beauty," *University of Western Ontario Medical Journal*, Fall 2011, vol. 80, no. 2, pp. 14–15. Copyright © 2011 by University of Western Ontario Medical Journal. All rights reserved. Reproduced by permission.

As you read, consider the following questions:

1. Why is the waist-to-hip ratio of women in the developed world an indicator of health status and fertility, according to Brichacek and Moreland?
2. What did the ancient Greeks believe was the ratio that defined facial beauty, as the authors explain?
3. In what way do the eleven separate meta-analyses explored by the authors strongly suggest that facial beauty is judged by a universal standard?

Our face allows us to convey our every thought and feeling with those around us in a nearly instantaneous manner. Without our face, we would be stuck in an emotionless and depressing self-existence devoid of a primary vehicle of communication. As social beings, it is in our very nature to share our expressions with the outside world. It is likewise in our nature to subconsciously judge each face, assigning certain traits to particular facial characteristics. One of the most important characteristics that we judge is "beauty". Interestingly, there is an unusually consistent agreement of what is considered "beautiful" amongst different cultures, but only when we are referring to the face rather than the body, a topic that will be explored herein.

The Beauty of the Body

So what is it that makes a person "beautiful"? Beauty is an arbitrary and abstract concept that is seemingly difficult, if not impossible to define. Considering the vast diversity in this world and the countless cultures it contains, one would expect that surely there must be different culturally dependent standards of beauty. However, research suggests that this is only partially correct.

Research examining the physical attractiveness of the female body often uses the waist-to-hip ratio (WHR) as a quantifiable measure. Indeed, studies have found that males from most cultures and across history strongly prefer female figures with a low WHR. In the developed world, healthy females have higher levels of estrogen that cause more fat to be deposited on the buttocks and hips rather than on the waist, leading to a low WHR. Thus, the WHR is an indicator of health status and fertility, and male preference for low-WHR females is considered an excellent example of male assessment of mate quality.

Despite the overall preference of men for women with a low WHR, variations do exist, thereby casting doubt on the theory that this may be a universal ideal. Another measure of body habitus[1] is the body mass index (BMI), which is a heuristic[2] proxy for human body fat. Different cultures and populations prefer females of different BMI and WHR due to different sociocultural influences. Undeniably, the effect of "Westernization" may be contributing to a more universal standard of beauty, but this is not due to our innate evolutionary preferences. Regardless of these influences, a study comparing female physical attractiveness between Japanese and British participants found that Japanese men preferred images of woman with significantly lower BMIs than Britons and likewise were more reliant on body shape when judging physical attractiveness.

The Influence of Western Media

However, the flaw with these studies in general is that every culture tested so far has been exposed to the potentially confounding influence of Western media. A landmark study by [D.W.] Yu and [G.H.] Shepard assessed the WHR preferences of a culturally isolated population of Matsigenka indigenous people in Peru, who are located in an extensive nature park where access is restricted solely to scientific and official visitors and the vast majority of natives have never left the premises. Their results showed that the WHR preferences of males of this tribe differed strikingly from those of the United States control population as well as from other world cultures, with the "over-weight" female ranking highest in the factors of attractiveness, healthiness, and preferred spouse.

"Now That You're 10, We Can Tell You the Truth: Beauty Isn't Actually in the Eye of the Beholder, There Are Standards . . . And You Haven't Met Them," cartoon by Guy and Rodd. www.CartoonStock.com.

These were critical findings as they differed strikingly from the preferences of males in other cultures. The authors suggest that this difference may be due to the fact that in traditional societies, physical features may play a lesser role because mate choice is limited by kinship rules, and potential mates have access to direct information about mate quality, such as age and history of illness. As a result, they do not rely primarily on information inferred from physical appearance. In contrast, in industrialized societies, daily exposure to strangers from an early age may increase the importance of using physical features to assess potential mates based on these factors.

Facial Beauty Is Rooted in Symmetry

It seems reasonable to question whether these relative cultural norms likewise influence our perception of facial beauty. Counterintuitively, the answer is no. Before exploring this topic, we must first consider what exactly facial beauty is and how to define it. The quest to find [a] suitable definition of facial beauty dates back to antiquity, when the ancient Greeks believed that beauty appeared when the ratio of many different facial features to each other approached the value 1:1.618, the so-called golden ratio. However, things are not so simple, as further research has shown that facial beauty is more a combination of symmetry and an ideal harmony of the facial features with each other. And most importantly, as humans we have an innate mechanism for detecting this elusive concept of beauty.

Symmetry is an important aspect of facial beauty and is tied to evolutionary fitness, where left-right bilateral symmetry describes health and high genetic quality, and deviations from it may indicate poor qualities and therefore form a basis for rejection of a potential mate.

There are several examples that seem to reinforce this concept. For instance, supermodels, arguably considered the most attractive members of Western society, have the least degree of facial asymmetry when compared to the general population. Facial asymmetry exists along a gradient in our population and it is clear that we have evolved to tolerate some degree of this asymmetry.

Average Is Beautiful

Interestingly, studies have shown that averaging a random group of faces results in a synthetic face more attractive than any of the original faces. The faces used in these analyses consisted of thirty-two completely random faces from a pool of different cultures, yet observers always ranked the composite face as being the most attractive. Paradoxically, this suggests that the ideal harmony of the facial features that we consider to be "beautiful" is actually as close to "average" as possible. Naturally, such statements have drawn criticism from many individuals who refuse to believe that beauty may in any way related to "averageness".

It is critical to note that the computational "average" of facial features that is considered attractive in this case is completely distinct from what culture commonly refers to as an "average" face, which naturally has a negative connotation and is not considered "beautiful". There are certainly unique and interesting features that may add to the perceived attractiveness of an individual's face, but it is important to realize that they must be associated with an "average" face and must be harmonious with the other facial features.

There have been arguments that beauty is a cultural phenomenon engrained in us repeatedly throughout our youth, resulting in a biased preference such as that of male for females with a low WHR ratio. However, there are many examples that disprove this theory. Eleven separate meta-analyses have revealed very high agreement in facial-attractiveness ratings by raters both within their own culture, and across other cultures. In fact, the effect sizes were more than double the size necessary to be considered large and thereby strongly suggest a universal standard by which facial attractiveness is judged.

In order to negate the possible influence of Western media, a study examining preferences for facial symmetry between British individuals and the Hazda, a hunter-gatherer society of Tanzania, likewise found that facial symmetry was more attractive than asymmetry across both cultures. These findings further question the assumption that ratings of facial attractiveness and ideals of facial "beauty" are culturally unique and are consistent with the fact that young infants prefer to look at faces that adults likewise consider to be attractive.

The Impact of Exogenous Factors

It is important to realize that there are exogenous factors that augment attractiveness and beauty as it pertains to mate selection, which is precisely why it is such an elusive concept to define. [D.] Dutton argues that based on Darwinian [i.e., evolutionary] aesthetics, individuals consciously select mates who have certain characteristics, and that such characteristics in fact may make the person more attractive and "beautiful" to them. Dutton further states that it is human personality that adds another dimension of beauty, with traits such as a delightful sense of humor and generosity being attractive. Although it is still evolutionarily based on finding a healthy mate who is able to provide care, it is this rational intention combined with physical appearance that forms a complete view of beauty and attractiveness.

Beauty is an elusive concept that is envied and sought by many, yet is extremely difficult to define. Although the beauty of the body has an evolutionary basis, the concept of the ideal body is a cultural construct that has been influenced and continues to be influenced by culture and media. Conversely, facial beauty is a biologically ingrained concept based on symmetry and an ideal coalescence of . . . facial features with each other that transcend barriers of culture, media, and time. Ultimately, concepts of beauty and attractiveness are evolutionarily based, but cannot be looked at narrowly as based solely on appearance as they are augmented by exogenous factors.

Notes

1. *Body habitus* is the medical term for physique and is defined as either endomorphic (overweight), ectomorphic (underweight) or mesomorphic (normal weight).
2. *Heuristic* refers to experience-based techniques for problem solving that are used where an exhaustive search is impractical or an exact answer is unnecessary. Examples include using a rule of thumb, an educated guess, an intuitive judgment, or common sense.

> "The media have . . . had an increasing
> influence on both the importance and
> definition of attractiveness."

Standards of Beauty Are Increasingly Influenced by the Media

Deborah L. Rhode

In the following viewpoint, Stanford University law professor Deborah L. Rhode argues that the media define beauty. Unfortunately, the resulting standards often reflect conflicting interests, she maintains. For example, Rhode claims, many women's magazines, dependent on advertising, establish beauty standards to promote beauty products, and makeover reality television shows suggest that anyone can be transformed into a beauty but do not reveal the risks of cosmetic surgery. Moreover, she maintains, media exposure to unattainable beauty ideals lowers self-esteem and increases body-image dissatisfaction. Sadly, Rhode reasons, even successful women face media scrutiny that focuses on appearance rather than on skills.

As you read, consider the following questions:

1. What does Rhode assert was the goal of the 1934 exposé *Skin Deep: The Truth About Beauty Aids?*

Deborah L. Rhode, "The Pursuit of Beauty," *The Beauty Bias: The Injustice of Appearance in Life and Law.* New York: Oxford University Press, 2010, pp. 45, 54–55, 58–65, 68. Copyright © 2010 by Oxford University Press. All rights reserved. Reproduced by permission.

2. What was the media response to Hillary Clinton during her political career, according to the author?

3. In the author's view, how do the media frame being overweight?

A widely circulated cartoon by Nicole Hollander features her main character, Sylvia, having a drink with a male friend. He wants her to "Admit it Syl. You need us. Can you imagine a world without men?" Her response: "No crime and lots of happy fat women." Underlying that quip are more serious questions about where our preoccupation with attractiveness comes from and what costs it imposes. To what extent are current standards a function of deeply rooted sexual drives, market forces, technological advances, or media pressures? Only by understanding what fuels our concerns about appearance can we effectively challenge their adverse consequences. . . .

Beauty Standards in Women's Magazines

The media have . . . had increasing influence on both the importance and definition of attractiveness. Although publications for women long included tips for "beautifying" products, their audience expanded significantly with the rise of women's magazines in the late nineteenth and early twentieth centuries. In these magazines, the lines between advice and advertisements have often blurred. Commentators have seldom been shy about endorsing products touted in ads, and sellers increasingly have demanded "compatible copy" surrounding their products. As early as 1934, a prominent exposé, *Skin Deep: The Truth about Beauty Aids*, called editors to task for peddling unnecessary and ineffectual products. For example, columnists who were in "kindly cooperation with the advertising department" declared it "quite improper [for women] to appear on the tennis court without a certain shade of nail polish," and insisted "that another is needed for cocktails, still another for the theatre."

Fashion, figures, food, and furnishings have been the main staples of women's magazines, and have often yielded ironic juxtapositions. Endless variations of the "last chance diet" have run back to back with recipes for "new ways to sin." A contemporary cover story on model Cybill Shepherd, "At Home with Cybill, and Yes, She's Lost 25 Pounds," featured not only diet tips but also a favorite dessert (toasted banana bread with ice cream).

A common refrain of these publications has been the importance of self-improvement. Estée Lauder captured the prevailing wisdom: "There are no homely women, only careless women. You have to want [beauty] very much and then help it along." The *Ugly-Girl Papers*, an 1875 collection from *Harper's Bazaar*, made a similar point in chapters titled "Women's Business to Be Beautiful," and "Hope for Homely People." One hundred and thirty-five years later, the basic message remains the same. A recent sample of leading women's magazines reveals cover features including: "Get a Sexy Body" (*Cosmopolitan*); "The Cost of Looking Good" (*Vogue*); "Swallow This: New Beauty Pills" (*Marie Claire*); "Look Younger by Morning" (*Harper's Bazaar*); "Wynonna's Weight Loss Secrets" (*Ladies' Home Journal*); "Easiest Ways to Lose 10lbs: No Diet, No Exercise, Seriously" (*Good Housekeeping*). Even niche magazines often have a liberal sprinkling of such assistance. Evangelicals get "Pray Your Weight Away," and "More of Jesus, Less of Me;" older women learn "Top Tricks to a Flawless Face" and "59 Ways to More Radiant Skin." . . .

The Influence of Reality Television

A related phenomenon involves reality television shows in which contestants either compete to lose weight (*The Biggest Loser, Celebrity Fit Club*) or receive full-body makeovers through diets, cosmetic surgery, hairstyling, and clothing (*The Swan, Extreme Makeover*). Before it expired in 2007, *Extreme Makeover* promised potential contestants "a truly Cinderella-like experience" in which they could transform their "life and destiny" and "make [their] dreams come true." Although male makeover candidates were welcome, they constituted only 4 percent of the applicant pool. And they have been excluded from other events that exalt such reconstructive efforts, such as a Miss Plastic Surgery contest, in which women from all nations vie to improve on nature. Here again, reality television's display of competition begins early. *Toddlers and Tiaras*, a TLC show, follows two-year-old pageant contestants as they "strut and swagger" with full makeup and styled hair.

This prime-time landscape is littered with irony. Surrounding weight-reduction contests are many of the very food advertisements that make the competitions necessary; Baskin-Robbins' Oreo sundaes and "all you can eat" breakfasts at Applebee's. These reality programs approximate "reality" in only the loosest sense. Editing omits anything that is not part of the "new and better you" story line: "bad results . . . complications, and lengthy recovery time." Watching these programs—the functional equivalent of "infomercials"—has been linked to lower self-esteem and higher dissatisfaction with body image, as well as greater desire for cosmetic surgery.

Exposure to Unattainable Ideals

Similar results occur from repeated exposure to fashion models and other celebrities who reflect increasingly unattainable ideals. Playwright Eve Ensler's *The Good Body* notes the influence of this "blond, pointy breast, raisin-a-day-stomached girl. . . . She is there every minute, somewhere in the world, smiling down on me, on all of us. She is omnipresent. She's the American Dream, my personal nightmare." A central problem involves weight. In 1894, the United States' average female model was 5 feet 4 inches tall and weighed 140 pounds. A century later, these proportions reflected the average American woman, but the average model was 5 feet 10 inches tall and 110 pounds, and she has been growing thinner ever since. Only 5 percent of American women are now in the same weight category as actresses and models. Comparable changes have occurred in other cultural icons. *Playboy* centerfolds have dropped in weight every year since the magazine began, and Miss Americas have followed suit. In top-rated prime-time television programs, overweight female characters seldom appear, and rarely in appealing roles. In women's health and fitness magazines, nonslender bodies are entirely absent, except as "before" pictures in successful weight-loss sagas. Yet as medical experts note, "[t]he current ideal of female beauty, a thin, well-toned, yet big-breasted woman—rarely occurs without restrictive dieting, excessive exercise, and cosmetic surgery." Women who internalize this ideal end up with unrealistic aspirations and unhealthy habits. About three quarters of women who are at or below normal weight believe that they should lose some.

For men, cultural expectations have traditionally been less demanding. However, male concerns have recently been increasing, partly in response to media messages. "Torch Your Bodyfat" and "Train Your Way to Megamass" are recurring refrains in men's magazines and advertisements. Male icons have grown larger and more muscular in virtually all media portrayals, except in fashion. There, designers have insisted that emaciation makes male as well as female models "look good in the clothes."

On the whole, however, the focus on weight reduction is much greater for women than for men. Articles and ads on weight loss in women's magazines have been rising as women's ideal weight has been falling; such magazines average about ten times as many diet advertisements and seven times as many diet articles as publications targeting men. Much of this material is unhelpful, unrealistic, and, for younger readers, unhealthy. "I Was a Hopeless Fatty, Now I'm a Model" has long been a dominant theme. Many studies show that frequent exposure to media images and diet articles is associated with heightened anxiety and unhappiness concerning appearance, as well as eating disorders, particularly in female adolescents.

The power of the media was dramatically illustrated by the introduction of television in Fiji in the 1990s. This was a culture that had long valued robust bodies and had almost no incidence of eating disorders. Within three years after television viewing became common, such disorders dramatically increased. Many female adolescents quickly became intent on replicating the figures they saw; "I want their body" was a common refrain. That desire is, of course, widely shared in Western countries such as the United States, where half of girls age nine to eighteen consider themselves fat and two-thirds of college-age women are dieting.

Unreasonable Standards Are Applied to Prominent Women

The media's focus on the appearance of prominent women reinforces these desires. [US secretary of state] Hillary Clinton is a textbook case. As first lady, she was ridiculed as "frumpy"; "Fashion stayed home" was a representative description of one of her European trips. During her Senate campaign, panelists on CNN's *Larry King Live* show described her as "fat," "bottom heavy," and "short legged." No one made even a pretense of explaining why her "bad figure" was relevant. During Clinton's presidential bid, her slight show of cleavage on the Senate floor merited *Washington Post* coverage, and [radio talk-show host] Rush Limbaugh asked his estimated fourteen million listeners whether Americans "will want to watch a woman get older before their eyes on a daily basis?"

If they don't, part of the reason is the absence of attractive older women in the media who actually look their age. Studies of film, television, and print media repeatedly find that older women are grossly underrepresented and rarely unreconstructed. News anchors such as Walter Cronkite and Tom Brokaw retain their influence, and male movie stars can play romantic leads well into their later years. In his sixties Sean Connery earned one of *People* magazine's annual awards for the "sexiest man alive." Women, by contrast, are expected to play opposite men thirty years their

The Psychological Impact of Media Exposure

Research has shown that media exposure to unattainable physical perfection is detrimental to people, especially women, and that the detrimental effects are currently more the rule than the exception. Women may directly model unhealthy eating habits presented in the media, such as fasting or purging, because the media-portrayed thin ideal body type is related to eating pathology. Media exposure to female images that are thin and air-brushed is also associated with depression and lower self-esteem in the women who view them.

There is clear evidence suggesting that the media's typical portrayal of women in advertisements has a negative effect on the way women feel about themselves.

Cheryl J. Haas, Laura A. Pawlow, Jon Pettibone, and Dan J. Segrist, College Student Journal, *June 2012.*

senior, and to bow out gracefully or have "work done" when the signs of age become pronounced. Even those who make the effort risk comments like the one from a *Boston Herald* columnist about an overly made-up politician: "There seemed to be something humiliating, sad, desperate and embarrassing about [Florida politician] Katherine Harris, a woman of a certain age trying too hard to hang on." The "certain age" was 43.

A No-Win Situation

Even when more skillfully managed, such refurbishing efforts reinforce implausible ideals. In commenting on an air-brushed, surgically enhanced image of a woman, "probably in her seventies," Betty Friedan noted, "She doesn't look old. The problem is, she doesn't look real either." *Boston Globe* columnist Ellen Goodman made a similar point about a photo of Elizabeth Taylor at sixty, "nipped, tucked, and lifted out of her peer group. . . . Looking 35 and holding." But the prevalence of such images only gives women "an extension on aging. They are not being given permission to age gracefully." The culture generally, and the media in particular, is "telling women they can be younger longer. It is not welcoming old women."

This special scrutiny of female appearance puts prominent women in a no-win situation: it penalizes them for caring too much or not enough and diverts attention from their qualifications and performance. The media had a field day with [2008 vice presidential candidate] Sarah Palin's Beehive Beauty Shop hairdo and the disconnect between her "hockey mom" rhetoric and $150,000 designer wardrobe, financed by the Republican National Committee. On Condoleezza Rice's first day as national security adviser, the *New York Times* ran a profile discussing her dress size (6), taste in shoes ("comfortable pumps"), and hemline preferences ("modest"). After becoming secretary of state, her appearance in high boots when visiting troops in Germany inspired portrayals as a dominatrix in political cartoons and comedy routines. San Diego mayor Donna Frye's change of hairstyle and makeup after her election earned her the nickname "surfer chick." Harriet Miers, President [George W.] Bush's White House counsel and unsuccessful candidate for a Supreme Court appointment, was described on Jon Stewart's *Daily Show* as a "friend of the president and a Talbot's [a retailer of classic clothing] frequent shopper."

The Intense Scrutiny of Women

Male candidates have also been on the receiving end of such treatment. Al Gore's weight and wardrobe choices were cause for comment, as were John Edward's $400 haircuts and John Kerry's possible Botox use. But the scrutiny of women is more intense, the standards more exacting, and the risks are greater of paying too much or not enough attention to their appearance. When Katie Couric became the first female anchor of network night-time news, the comments on her image were unremitting. Many wondered whether she was up to the job or had gotten it for the "right reasons." After all, noted the *New York Times*, "Unless CBS designs a new anchor desk, Ms. Couric's well-toned legs will no longer be on prominent display." In fact, when Couric had briefly substituted for Jay Leno several years earlier, the network staff cut a hole in the desk to expose her legs.

Yet women who have all the substantive qualifications for such a position, but lack the right age, ethnicity, or "look," face even greater hurdles. When a female meteorologist lost her position on a weather show for appearing too "matronly" and "dowdy," television host Conan O'Brien described her problem as "partly saggy with a chance of menopause."

Recognition of these disabling stereotypes seems part of what prompted the extraordinary outpouring of support for British singer Susan Boyle. Some 114 million viewers replayed her performance on England's *You've Got Talent*. As *Ms.* editor Letty Pogrebin suggested, what moved many of them to tears may have been the "years of wasted talent, the career that wasn't. . . . If someone with a voice like Julie Andrews spent decades in a sea of frustration and obscurity [because she didn't look the part], how many other women (and men) must be out there . . . in the same boat?"

Even the most successful celebrities can be hobbled by our cultural obsession with appearance. On a 2009 cover of her magazine, a full-sized Oprah [Winfrey] looks at a re-creation of her trim 2005 body and asks, "How did I let this happen again?" In the story inside, one of the world's most successful entrepreneurs confesses that she felt "completely defeated" by her hardly atypical experience of yo-yo dieting. "I give up. Fat wins."

Fat Is Framed as Failure

Such mea culpas [confessions of fault] are consistent with most media portrayals, which frame fat as a failure of personal responsibility and a sign of moral laxity. Such accounts are partly responsible for the assumptions . . . that overweight individuals are too lazy to exercise and too self-indulgent to diet. Occasionally there are other villains in the story. The fast-food industry exploits our weaknesses, invades our schools, and blocks appropriate policy responses; technology spawns "telly tubbies" and "couch potatoes"; and feminism encourages "careerism," which leaves working women with too little time to provide home-cooked meals and to ensure healthy lifestyles for their children. No one faults working fathers.

The Coverage of Female Athletes

A final example of the media's preoccupation with appearance and sexual double standards involves the coverage of female athletes. Those who are attractive receive vastly disproportionate attention, and much of it highlights sex rather than sports. A study of *Sports Illustrated* found that only 10 percent of the photos were of women, and half of those were in provocative poses. Many female Olympic athletes manage to achieve coverage only in the swimsuit issue. The alluring Anna Kournikova received an eight-page spread in the magazine and became the highest-earning female tennis player in the world without ever winning a professional singles tournament. The far-less-photogenic Wimbledon winner, Lindsay Davenport, got barely a mention. Playboy.com has featured "babes of the LPGA [Ladies Professional Golf Association]," and *Gear* magazine pictured Brandi Chastain wearing only her soccer cleats, balancing soccer balls on her breasts and crotch. Even the normally staid *New York Times Sunday Magazine* offered a sexualized photo spread of the Russian women's tennis team under the title "Court-esans." For these women, one portrayed with racket, spike heels, and a low-cut "Louis Vuitton minidress," the subtitle ran "love is just another four letter word." "How practical is a stiletto on the court?" asked the photo caption. Answer from Anna Chakvetadze: "Those heels would destroy the courts." But who cares? Product endorsements often take a similar tack. Anna Kournikova's Berlei Bra ad ran under the slogan, "Only the balls should bounce."

Defenders of such displays claim that they benefit women's sports by appealing to potential male viewers and dispelling any stereotypes that make strength and sweat seem unfeminine. But if so, the price is to objectify athletes who deserve the attention on other grounds and to suggest that, whatever their accomplishments, their sexual appeal matters just as much. Male athletes encounter no such expectations. No one is posing Tiger Woods with golf balls foregrounding his crotch. . . .

The Culture of Beauty

"Should we try to learn to live with what we are left with?" wonders Doris Grumbach in her memoir of aging, *Coming into the End Zone*. Contemporary Western societies make that difficult. Our genes, history, and market structures are stacked against it. A $200 billion global industry is heavily invested in fueling anxieties over appearance and a need for self-improvement. Technological advances have expanded our opportunities, and media images are an ever-present reminder of the gap between our aspirations and achievements. Our appearance is in constant need of renovation, and our spiffed-up selves need a wide range of commercial assistance to keep them that way.

Although some of the effort can be satisfying, it can also be an unwelcome burden and a source of shame, frustration, and unnecessary expense. Particularly for women, the priority we place on appearance presents ongoing challenges, with profound personal as well as political dimensions.

"*Body hatred and body anxiety . . .
[are] the emotional fallout from
the endeavours of [Western beauty]
industries and the basis on which they
make their extraordinary and obscene
profits.*"

Market Principles Foster Dangerous Standards of Beauty

Susie Orbach

In the following excerpt from a speech delivered during a meeting of the United Nations Commission on the Status of Women, British psychotherapist and social critic Susie Orbach asserts that beauty industries create unrealistic beauty standards to profit from body hatred. Because of their market power, cosmetic companies, fashion houses, and the diet industry have so narrowed what is beautiful that women and girls resort to destructive practices such as self-starvation and surgery, she claims. To decry violence against women in the developing world while tolerating these self-destructive practices among Western women is hypocritical,

Orbach reasons. Nevertheless, she maintains, people allow these
industries to market body hatred across the globe.

As you read, consider the following questions:
1. According to Orbach, how is individual beauty now judged?
2. Why does the author maintain that taking on any of
   the beauty industries will be as challenging as taking on
   tobacco?
3. Why is the global spread of the beauty industry the new
   frontier of colonialism, in the author's opinion?

It has been customary for the West to bemoan and critique the
appalling forms of violence practiced against girls and women
in the rest of the world—FGM [female genital mutilation], rape
as a tactic of war, forced marriage.

Violence Against Western Female Bodies

In this focus what has been overlooked have been the vicious
body practices that girls and women have come to take on themselves in the West in the mistaken belief that they are doing good
for themselves.

These include:
- Self-starvation and the often bulimic response—compulsive
  eating and vomiting
- The surgical transformation of breasts, legs, stomachs,
  cheek bones to conform to the latest beauty ideal
- The use of diet and pharmaceutical products to suppress
  appetite
- The botoxing of 5 year olds

The West congratulates itself on its distance from Eastern
practices of foot binding which constrained and limited women.
It fails to see the links between toe operations carried out now to
enable women to fit into the latest 4 inch high heels.

The West smugly criticises FGM while sanctioning labia-plasty and the remaking of the genital lips which has become a growth area for cosmetic surgeons.

The West makes appeals about famine victims in the southern hemisphere but has failed to notice the voluntarily insane food practices that exist in their own countries.

Explaining Western Attitudes

The West hasn't noticed that these are forms of violence and constraint for women. And they haven't noticed for three important reasons.

The first is that the idea of beauty has been democratised—extended to all. The second is that simultaneously, the ideal of what beauty is has narrowed.

Beauty is no longer seen as intrinsic to the individual. Instead the individual is judged on how well she can shape herself to today's aesthetic, which is tall, white, blonde, long-haired and big breasted.

The imperative of beauty traverses class and age. From 5 to 80, girls and women learn they need to look at themselves from the outside *whatever* they are doing to make sure they look good. This demand can produce severe anguish, self-alienation, eating problems, body distortions and disturbing mental health issues.

Growing Rich on Body Hatred

The third reason is connected to the other two in significant ways. It is the engine which feeds the tyrannical hold that beauty exercises on girls and women's energies, dollars and sense of self. It relates to those industries which grow rich on creating body distress and body hatred in girls and women.

These industries look like they are benevolent and helpful. In fact they are quite the opposite.

The beauty companies, the fashion houses, the diet companies, the food conglomerates who also of course own the diet

Creative Marketing Strategies

The market in cosmetic procedures has grown over 400 percent in just the last decade, spurred by ever more creative marketing strategies: "surgeon and safari" getaway vacations and Botox house parties, with a physician on hand to inject the guests. Los Angeles' Aesthetica offers the "perfect" "Say It with Liposuction" Valentine's Day gift "for the woman who has everything." This "ultimate cosmetic surgery experience" comes complete with stretch limousine travel, a twenty-four-hour private nurse, Dior robe, Godiva chocolate, and the "fixative" procedure of her choice.

Deborah L. Rhode, The Beauty Bias, *2010.*

companies, the exercise and fitness industry, the pharmaceutical industry, and the cosmetic surgery industry combine together—perhaps not purposefully or conspiratorially—to create a climate in which girls and women come to feel that their bodies are not OK. They do this through the promotion of celebrity culture, through advertising on every possible outlet from billboards to magazines to our electronic screens, through the funding of media outlets which can only exist because of their economic support.

Taking on any one of these industries is difficult and will pose the same kind of challenges as taking on tobacco who also portrayed themselves as health giving and benevolent. The profits of WW's [Weight Watchers] for example were up 25.3% in 2011. We are talking big money. We are talking about a company whose product needs to fail in order for it to keep selling. If dieting worked you would only have to do it once. There would be no repeat customers.

Marketing Western Bodies

As immoral and unethical as the activities of these companies are in and of themselves, the economics of growth as we currently conceive it depends upon their extending their markets. L'Oréal's growth rate in China is 26%. They achieve this not by marketing their lipsticks and hair products to Chinese women per se but by marketing the western body as *the body* to have to Chinese women. They and the other beauty, fashion, media companies promote the western body to the new economies as a way of finding a place to belong in the maelstrom and confusion of modernity.

Alongside the disseminating of western ideals of beauty to Asia, Africa and South America, is the export of the consequences of these ideals: body hatred and body anxiety. This is the emotional fallout from the endeavours of these industries and the basis on which they make their extraordinary and obscene profits.

This is a not an easy target to attack. These industries are not small and their damage is great. *They are mining bodies as though they were a commodity like coal or gold.* Women's bodies all over the world are being designated as profit centres.

As the western ideal becomes plastered over the globe we bear witness to the loss of indigenous bodies. This is a new frontier of colonialism. Mad eating is normalised. Western style bodies are revered and local bodies are swallowed up as fast as the demise of local languages. We must stop it. And now.

| *"The 'economy of sameness' [is] yoking all cultures to the same idea of beauty which is linked to assimilating all countries into the same economic model."* |

Western Standards of Beauty Have Spread via Globalization

Yasmin Alibhai-Brown

The worldwide expansion of trade and communication also expands unrealistic Western beauty ideals and the psychological problems that accompany them, argues Yasmin Alibhai-Brown in the following viewpoint. For example, she maintains, women from cultures that once celebrated curvy figures are now obsessed with being skinny or surgically changing the shape of their eyes. An economic model that allows companies to promote perfection and create global body dissatisfaction is unethical, Alibhai-Brown claims. Moreover, she asserts, the constant assault of Western images leads to a loss of cultural self-expression. Alibhai-Brown is a Ugandan-born British journalist and commentator for the Independent, *a London newspaper.*

As you read, consider the following questions:

1. According to Alibhai-Brown, why had no African woman ever won Miss World until 2000?

2. Before constant bombardment from the media and beauty industry, from where did pressure on women about how they should look come, in the author's view?

3. What did an anonymous scientist tell the author is the grand plan of a famous cosmetic firm?

Five years ago [in 2005], Kareena Kapoor, a top young actress in Bollywood [the movie industry in India], was a typical Punjabi girl, buxom and shapely, luscious like sweet kulfi ice-cream. Today, I imagine, kulfi would make her heave and biryani [a traditional Indian dish] is never on her plate. For, you see, Kareena saw the light, and today she is svelte and sinewy enough to jog on the streets of LA and wear the tightest of designer jeans. Her millions of fans have gone crazy, they speculate on the web about her amazing diet and want to copy her example. Size zero has arrived in India.

The singer Katy Perry went [traditional] Indian for her wedding to the comedian Russell Brand, but sophisticated Indian women want to be like her before the makeover. Reena, a Mumbai make-up artist I spoke to is scathing. "Silly girl, Katy, going for retro like that. Elephants and garish colours—really, how low class! Makes us look so backward. Really, don't they know we are modernising? Our designers and models could be on catwalks in Paris and Milan now. We got the message." And how.

Student Mika Bhatia, 21, a Californian of Indian origin says urban India is cutting off from its own history and ways of life recklessly and hastily: "Fifteen years ago the American influence was absent and women would dress in their traditional clothes, look great. Now it is all about Western clothes. It's sad. It's happening so fast. I notice it every time I go back." You can see similar trends in other developing nations and emerging markets. Globalisation shrinks the world in more ways than we think.

The Skinny Trend

Sophie Kafeero was my roommate at university in Uganda, a wonderfully vivacious African woman with a curvy body, pursued by male students. "It wouldn't happen today she tells me. Young women who want to be popular 'showcase' girlfriends are skinny, have to be." One young woman at a local internet cafe so didn't want to be like her large mother, she has become anorexic. Quacks offer Chinese potions to get weight off. Business is booming.

Ugandan British solicitor [lawyer] Jennifer Nyeko Jones confirms these trends: "The old posters are slowly fading—when large women were admired because it meant they were living well. Western men who go to Africa looking for girls are bringing this idea too. African men are not asking for it. Gyms are now everywhere, taking the place of popular local beauty parlours."

Until 2000, no African woman had ever won Miss World, mainly because the nations selected big lovelies with sassy walks, like the fictional lady detective, Precious Ramotswe, of Alexander McCall Smith's Botswana novels. Then in 2001, a Western scout found the Nigerian Agbani Darego, tall, slim, small nose, large eyes, shiny skin. She was duly crowned and became the new ideal beauty. AIDS is known as the "slim disease" across the continent. Now another slim disease has arrived.

Elsewhere the demand is for altered features. South Korean women have their eyes de-orientalised for $800. In Singapore the men too opt for surgery, like the stylist Alvin Goh, who says he now fits better into the fashion industry. More nose jobs are done in Iran than any other country on earth. In his project "Love Me," about the global beauty industry, the British photographer Zed Nelson [in 2009] raised the spectre of an "eerily homogenised" world, dull and samey like a prairie.

Along with goods and services, neuroses are also being exported, from us in the West to them in the rest of the world. In the age of exploration Europeans unknowingly introduced their diseases into populations which had no immunity to protect them. The viruses now transmitted abroad are carried on the backs of unbridled consumerism and free enterprise.

We need to face up to what that has done to our own societies and debate the ethics of the economic model that creates misery and dissatisfaction and cashes in on it. And then ask ourselves by what right we inflict the same and worse on other civilizations.

Peddlers of Physical Perfection

Western women are programmed and controlled by the peddlers of physical perfection even though from time to time we like to imagine we have pulled ourselves free. Take Christina Hendricks, the stupendously voluptuous Joan Holloway in [the AMC TV series] *Mad Men*, apparently the nemesis of zealous body regulators who only exalt females with lovely bones and small, pert, boobs. Hers are prodigious knockers, and then there's the door-sized bum and that animal walk, inviting and yet mean. Propping her up and out, though, are engineering miracles and feminine suffering we can but imagine. Fashionistas are ordering corsets with padded seats from Rio; Prada frocks pay homage to her shape and *Esquire* crowns her the "best looking woman in America." The equalities minister Lynne Featherstone believes the actress is a "fabulous" role model and is setting up discussions with people from the fashion and media industries to get them to change models from little to large and boost female confidence. But for these merchants small is bountiful, brings in mega profits. Women with meat on them are unsightly, no good as bait. True, public effusion breaks out seasonally when, on TV, Nigella [Lucy Lawson, a British TV food broadcaster] invites millions to drool over her puddings. Beth Ditto and Ruth Jones from the popular series *Gavin and Stacy*, and dear old Ann Widdecombe [a British politician and author] are fat and proud but the appeal for most is freakish. The idolatry of Hendricks too is more hope than expectation. Like a modern day Botticelli [a Renaissance artist] maiden, she rises out of the sea, briefly, before going under again.

Upholders of beauty exploit the inadequacies of a weak and needy post-modern society that must be told what to be. The exceptions above can't overturn the rules. Smart, successful, aspirational people are lean or must try to be.

From Concern to Obsession

The scale and penetration of such messaging in modern times is unprecedented. Academic Kate Fox of the Social Issues Research Centre warned way back in 1998: "Advances in technology have caused normal concerns about how we look to become obsessions . . . we have become accustomed to rigid and uniform standards of beauty . . . on TV billboards and magazines, we see 'beautiful people' all the time, more often than members of our own family, making exceptional good looks seem real, normal and attainable."

For the comedian and writer Arabella Weir this trickery leads to perpetual dissatisfaction: "The celeb culture holds up the thin look, rarefied and glamorous women and at the same time it invites us to see them as ordinary—we can have a life just like them. See Cheryl Cole [a British popular music artist]? We can buy copies of her shoes and be her." Except we can't.

You could argue that every age has beauty prototypes and evanescence is the handmaiden of capitalism. Women have been made to conform to templates within all social systems. The horrendous corsets of the Victorian era broke their bodies and girdles of the Fifties severely controlled the feminine form. Then the corsets became mental. Weir's poignant new book, *The Real Me Is Thin* describes how her parents, both academics, believed girls had to be thin, "to please men, to be fantasised about." The child was forbidden pudding, the extra potato. Her mother said watching Arabella eat was like having hot knives poked into her eyes. Most

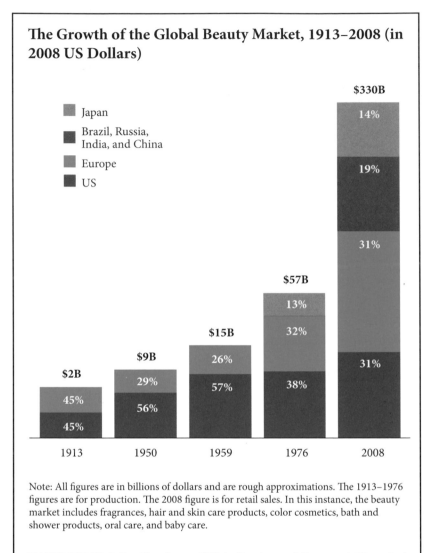

The Growth of the Global Beauty Market, 1913–2008 (in 2008 US Dollars)

Japan

Brazil, Russia, India, and China

Europe

US

$330B
14%
19%
31%
31%

$57B
13%
32%
38%

$15B
26%
57%

$9B
29%
56%

$2B
45%
45%

1913   1950   1959   1976   2008

Note: All figures are in billions of dollars and are rough approximations. The 1913–1976 figures are for production. The 2008 figure is for retail sales. In this instance, the beauty market includes fragrances, hair and skin care products, color cosmetics, bath and shower products, oral care, and baby care.

TAKEN FROM: Geoffrey Jones, "Globalization and Beauty: A Historical and Firm Perspective," *EurAmerica*, vol. 41, no. 4, December 2011, p. 888.

young women interviewed for her book confessed they would not have dessert on a first date. Gluttony puts men off, they fear.

However, even until the late Nineties, the idea of beauty was not squeezed into one thin tube. Stars could still come in different shapes and sizes. The supermodels of the 1980s were strong-looking and broad-shouldered. Before that, Audrey Hepburn and Twiggy were thought stunning, so too Ava Gardener, Liz Taylor, Sophia Loren and Marilyn Monroe. In 2010, even the shapely Liz Hurley seems too fleshy; model Lara Stone (size 8) is thought daringly "curvy" and dream girl Cheryl Cole has melted down to size zero, the official size for the young, female and lionized. Kareena Kapoor is only following the new cosmopolitan aesthetics.

Variety Is No Longer Accepted

Thousands of years ago, Plato tried to codify facial attractiveness and, since then, researchers into beauty have found that symmetry and certain features have universal appeal. But to offset homogeneity is that other evolutionary imperative—variety. In his *Descent of Man*, [naturalist Charles] Darwin asserted: "It is certainly not true that there is in the mind of man any universal standard of beauty with respect to the human body. It is, however, possible that certain tastes, in the course of time, become inherited."

Anorexic chic has gone way beyond inherited taste; it ensnares millions, imperils the future itself. Intelligent women feel caught in the vice. As Mika Bhatia says: "There's such an obsession with being skinny. I wish I could say that I am removed from all of that but I don't think I am. I have always felt I had to work on my appearance and stay thin even though I know what can happen. A close female relative who was at UCLA [University of California, Los Angeles] has developed an eating disorder." Bhatia's family are the new globetrotters, with the gain that brings and tragic losses too.

Dutch literature undergraduate Mia De Graf, 19, grapples with the same dilemmas: "It's so mundane, having this single idea of beauty across the world, also so detrimental to our mental health. I am never repulsed when I see old paintings of women with larger figures, but it is weird because now, you think, someone like that should go to Weight Watchers. Take the [Dante] Rossetti painting [*Lady*] *Lillith*, she is absolutely beautiful but today her figure is too full to be beautiful."

Maria, 20, a nursery school assistant, daughter of Greek Cypriot migrants, who looks like Bridget Jones, is so sick of being on diets she is on anti-depressants instead: "How does Renée Zellweger [the actress who portrayed the pudgy Bridget Jones] get all that weight off and I can't? I have even written to her to ask. I hate myself, just a f--king failure. Look! Even my hands are fat. I can't wear a thong—my tush is too fat." Her nails are bitten right down and bleeding. Such deep misery in one fresh and lovely as a pink peach. A poet might once have written about her bloom, but such beauty has no place in our times.

These distorted values are dysphoric for all women. For British Asians, these images had not, until recently, infected our eyes, nor narrowed our tastes. There is among us an abhorrent acceptance of skin colour hierarchies in which light is best. But on the whole, we managed to avoid the brainwashing. The models and actresses didn't look like us so we could ignore them. Not any more.

Soni, a teenage British Asian girl, whose name means lovely, can't bear to look at herself. Alexa Chung [model and TV personality] struts through her dreams. Her mother fears her daughter is going mad. Only as mad as most other girls of her age: "Why can't she like herself? At 48 I think I look good, a little fat maybe, but so what? Even my mother likes her face. But not Soni, my rose, born here. In my village back home, I looked in the rivers and thought my face was so pretty. Soni says she will have operations one day." Many of our daughters are in similar crises.

Dangerous Cultural Shifts

These are momentous and dangerous cultural shifts, warns psychotherapist Gabrielle Rifkind: "Pressure on women as to how they should look came from different forms—from family, partners and friends. Now, it is the constant bombardment from the media and beauty industry, and this leads to a reduction in their ability to be independent of thought and creative in their own forms of self expression—the autonomy of the mind. The sexualisation of their image, expressed by very tight clothes and exposure of the body has accentuated a deep experience of alienation from the body, as expressed in rapid increase of anorexia and obesity."

A decade ago, writer Naomi Wolf foresaw the coming blight in her seminal book, *The Beauty Myth*. She was subjected to extraordinary vitriol for exposing the dark side of the beauty business. She lost; they won. The most unachievable images of pulchritude [beauty] are pressed into female psyches so they spend and cry. Natasha Walter, author of *Living Dolls*, a book on young women today, admits feminists should have been more vigilant: "I used to be blasé about beauty myths. It was the concrete stuff that mattered—jobs equality and all that. Now I can see how these industries fed into insecurities, spread a punishing view of what it means to be aspirational, the idea of failure. Its impact is huge." Especially, she says, among bright, ambitious girls in sixth form colleges [similar to a US junior college]. When she was young, "You could choose your persona and style. It was cool to look as if you weren't trying too hard, to be eccentric." She did find that contemporary black women were happier with their bodies and own individual choices. (Good hair for them, though, as Chris Rock's 2009 candid film of the same name showed, is straight and light, and many go through hell to get that look.)

Similarly, a study carried out in 2002 . . . compared the self images of Latin, black and white women. Although all groups agreed on what is thought to be perfect—white, slim, tall, straight noses—black women did not let that affect their self-esteem. White and Latino women in contrast felt they did not match up.

The Globalisation of Beauty

Some emerging economies seem frightfully keen on those manufactured images of perfection. Nonita Karla, editor-in-chief of

Elle India is delighted that her readers want to join the dubious club: "Indians have a more international concept of beauty," she says, "And we are now more in sync with global views and values, now it is an established fact. There is a global standard of beauty which is very western influenced, but local ideals live on, side by side."

Geoffrey Jones, author of *The History of the Global Beauty Industry* is less blasé: "The globalisation of mega, celebrity, and luxury brands provides compelling evidence of the 'flattening' of the world. These brands are the carriers of the latest trends, which companies now seem to be able to spread around the world, regardless of cultural traditions, ethnicity or income levels." This latest rush carries on from the periods of industrialisation and empire when white beauty norms were transplanted to colonised lands. Before then, says Jones, "Human societies had their own beauty ideals which differed sharply from one another."

A scientist who asked to remain anonymous tells me his famous cosmetic firm has a grand plan: "Like tobacco companies they are going hard for third-world markets, creating a dependent consumer class, gullible enough to believe the slick campaigns and polished lies. It makes me sick." Old tastes cannot survive such determined onslaughts.

I loved the old Bollywood actresses, graceful, bosomy and wide with soft bellies. With saris you cannot corset or hide much, nor did they try. Age did not bother them either, stars like Meena Kumari, Rakhi, Waheeda Rehman. To many young British women interviewed for this article the actresses are "gross," "overweight," "outdated." Most urban Indians would concur. Such a terrible shame that, especially in an old land which we know, from cave sculptures, paintings and the erotic *Kama Sutra* [a book on developing spirituality through sexuality], celebrated the infinite diversity of the Indian female form.

In her book *Images of the Modern Woman in Asia*, Shoma Munshi writes: "Up until the 1980s it was fine to be well rounded and voluptuous and films and advertisements of the time reflect this. . . . [Now] the Indian cinema and adverts [advertisements] reflect the arrival of the perfectly sculpted body to meet exacting international standards." It is, she believes, to do with a vast and growing middle class (125 million so far) who "swing between their Indian traditions and an internalised transnational identity more in keeping with global lifestyles."

Efforts to Resist

And as with Starbucks, the reach is infinite, though some are managing to resist the lure of the West. Just. In parts of Africa and Arabia female beauties can have big hips, bellies and breasts. The pernicious word "perfect" has not yet entered their lexicon. I asked Jemima Khan if she saw middle class Pakistan succumbing: "The country is more conservative than India, particularly in terms of fashion and dress. The shalwar khameez is designed to conceal a woman's figure. My sister-in-law, for example, hid her pregnancy until a week before giving birth. I couldn't tell even though I was living with her. Having said that, I interviewed a top model/actress there recently and yes she was minute, the Western ideal." Jemima's friend Suhair Khan believes change is unavoidable: "India is much more affected by globalisation but girls in Pakistan are now becoming conscious of being the 'right' size, everyone from my own friends to the manicure girl in Karachi. Those curvy film actresses are quite obviously a dying breed."

The only rebellion against this hegemony, believes Rifkind, is: "the rise of enveloped clothing expressed through the burkha, hijab, niqab—veiling—which could be seen as protection against the power of the beauty industry." For us feminists that response also negates selfhood and exerts conformity, pain without real gain.

More encouraging is how China manages modernity, says Livia Wang, an Anglo-Chinese teenager: "There was definitely a time when students dyed their hair and wore blue contact lenses, but as China opens up economically, I feel the richer classes are returning to more traditional ideas of beauty—maybe pre-communist imperial times. China is quite proud—they have their own movie and pop stars they look up to. So no I don't think the anxieties of western women are being imported." But they may in the end not be able to hold out.

The Economy of Sameness

"There is an explicit correlation between the emergence of so-called 'international looks' and the opening up of the economy to multinational corporations from the west," says Cambridge academic Priyamvada Gopal. "Two Indian women won world beauty titles in the Nineties—Aishwarya Rai and Sushmita Sen. Their arrival on the pageant stage symbolised the arrival of India on the world stage as an economic power to be reckoned with. It's what some scholars call the 'economy of sameness' yoking all cultures to the same idea of beauty which is linked to assimilating all countries into the same economic model."

And the same mental disintegration. Young Soni is now self harming and starving herself. On her wall she has posters of Keira Knightley and Kareena Kapoor, the beautiful looked up to by a new generation of the damned in the globalised world.

Periodical and Internet Sources Bibliography

The following articles have been selected to supplement the diverse views presented in this chapter.

Beauty Redefined	"How Girls and Women Can Take Back Beauty," February 17, 2011. www.beautyredefined.net.
Tan Choe Choe	"What Men Want in a Woman," *New Straits Times* (Malaysia), August 15, 2010. www.nst.com.my.
Leslie Leyland Fields	"The Power and the Glamour: Searching for Beauty and Hollywood's Beautiful People," *Christianity Today*, July 2011.
Thomas Gizbert	"What Makes a Pretty Face? The Biological Basis of Beauty," *Triple Helix Online* (blog), September 28, 2011. http://triplehelixblog.com.
Cheryl J. Haas, Laura A. Pawlow, Jon Pettibone, and Dan J. Segrist	"An Intervention for the Negative Influence of Media on Body Esteem," *College Student Journal*, June 2012.
Anne Kingston	"The Birth of Botox Feminism," *Maclean's*, January 18, 2010.
Nation	"Be 'Beautiful' and Be Damned," April 26, 2012.
Rick Nauert	"Body Image Often Based on Others' Opinion," Psych Central, March 29, 2012. http://psych central.com.
Ronda Racha Penrice	"Nicki Minaj and 'Marilyn Monroe': Is She Perpetuating White Female Beauty Standard?," The Grio, February 7, 2012. http:// thegrio.com.
Constance C.R. White	"Our Own Standards of Beauty," *Essence*, November 2011.
Lara Williams	"Some Body to Love," *The F Word*, June 2009. www.thefword.org.uk.

CHAPTER 2

What Impacts Do Ideals of Beauty Have on Society?

Chapter Preface

Consumer behavior analysts assert that more and more people are trying to slow the aging process. For example, forty-one-year-old Cheryl Hoover, in an effort to smooth wrinkles around her eyes and restore smoothness to her skin, has turned to Botox, collagen, and laser treatments. She explains, "I try to be proactive in heading off things. You want, as you get older, to appear youthful or at least look your age and not older. Our generation is looking for the fountain of youth."[1] In a society obsessed with youth, aging adults represent a significant target group for the beauty industry. In fact, research by Global Industry Analysts reveals that the market for antiaging products will grow from $80 billion in 2011 to more than $114 billion by 2015. Beauty industry advertisements promise that the signs of aging can indeed be eliminated. Thus, many older Americans hope to eliminate lines on their face with Botox and stretch sagging skin with plastic surgery. One of the controversies in the debate over the impact that ideals of beauty have on society is whether beauty standards that suggest that aging is something to be avoided and feared pose a threat to people as they age. While some claim that the fight against aging is a positive step, others claim that the pursuit of youth is costly, ineffective, and sometimes dangerous.

Antiaging advocates assert that the challenges associated with normal aging are treatable. In its mission statement, the American Academy of Anti-Aging Medicine maintains that the problems of aging "are caused by physiological dysfunction which in many cases are ameliorable to medical treatment." The organization claims that critics represent health and pharmaceutical industries that are threatened by antiaging industry profits. "It has to do with who's controlling the dollars,"[2] claims academy co-founder Robert Goldman. Even some anti-aging industry critics support cosmetic surgery as long as the patient is aware of the limits of what surgery can do. Case Western Reserve

University School of Medicine professor Robert Binstock told a friend whose spirits lifted after getting plastic surgery, "If you feel better looking in the mirror in the morning, fine." He told reporter David Crary, "I have no objection to people being narcissistic."[3]

Mainstream organizations such as the National Institute on Aging and many physicians warn aging Americans to be skeptical of costly and ineffective anti-aging products and procedures. "Despite claims about pills or treatments that lead to endless youth, no treatments have been proven to slow or reverse the aging process,"[4] the institute claims. University of Illinois–Chicago School of Public Health professor and aging expert S. Jay Olshansky warns, "If someone is promising you today that you can slow, stop or reverse aging, they're likely trying hard to separate you from your money."[5] Nevertheless, the American Society of Plastic Surgeons reports that in the United States, surgeons performed 13.1 million cosmetic procedures in 2010, a 77 percent increase from the beginning of the decade. Indeed, an Associated Press–LifeGoesStrong.com poll found that one in five baby boomers, those born between 1946 and 1964, have had or would consider cosmetic surgery. While treatment with the wrinkle-smoothing drug Botox may cost approximately four hundred dollars per treatment, a facelift can cost from six thousand to fifteen thousand dollars. However, while the noninvasive Botox is less costly, the effects will not last as long and may require repeated treatments. Dr. Peter Schmid, a surgeon on the board of the American Academy of Cosmetic Surgery, cautions patients to consider their options carefully. "There's a certain vulnerability because everybody's looking for that quick-fix, that fountain of youth," Schmid claims, and "many people will shop emotionally instead of objectively."[6] As an alternative to expensive and unproven antiaging products, Olshansky suggests, "invest in yourself, in the simple things we know work. Get a good pair of running or walking shoes and a health club membership, and eat more fruits and vegetables."[7]

Whether the culture of youth helps or hurts older Americans continues to be hotly contested. The authors in the following chapter present their views on similar controversies in answer to the question, what impact do ideals of beauty have on society? Whether in years to come growing older is celebrated or feared remains to be seen.

Notes

1. Delft I. Hawkins, David L. Mothersbaugh, and Roger J. Best, *Consumer Behavior*. Boston: McGraw-Hill Irwin, 2010.
2. Quoted in David Crary, "Boomers Will Be Spending Billions to Counter Aging" Associated Press, August 22, 2011. http://news.yahoo.com.
3. Quoted in Crary, "Boomers Will Be Spending Billions to Counter Aging."
4. Quoted in Crary, "Boomers Will Be Spending Billions to Counter Aging."
5. Quoted in Crary, "Boomers Will Be Spending Billions to Counter Aging."
6. Quoted in Crary, "Boomers Will Be Spending Billions to Counter Aging."
7. Quoted in Crary, "Boomers Will Be Spending Billions to Counter Aging."

> *"A focus on women's physical attributes means that their other attributes . . . are devalued."*

Women Are Judged on Their Appearance Rather than on Their Competence

Natasha Walter

Society determines a woman's status on the basis of her appearance, not the value of her work, claims Natasha Walter in the following viewpoint. For example, she asserts, commentators cruelly criticize women in political life if they do not meet standards of beauty and reduce them to sexual objects when they do. Successful women must tolerate this abuse as part of public life, Walter maintains. To question the focus on a woman's appearance is to question the power of the market, where what sells is more important than the ethics involved, she concludes. Walter, a British print and broadcast journalist, is author of Living Dolls.

As you read, consider the following questions:

1. What evidence does Walter provide that women still do not have the equality in politics that they have long sought?

Natasha Walter, "Choices," *Living Dolls: The Return of Sexism*. London, England: Virago, an imprint of Little, Brown Book Group, 2010, pp. 119–125. Copyright © 2010 by Virago. All rights reserved. Reproduced by permission.

2. How does the author describe the sexual bullying of Sarah Palin?
3. What did the author discover when she interviewed girls who were aiming for degrees and good careers?

The highly sexualised culture around us is tolerated and even celebrated because it rests on the illusion of equality. Since the idea has taken hold that women and men are now equal throughout society, it is seen as unproblematic that women should be relentlessly encouraged to prioritise their sexual attractiveness. The assumption is that this is a free choice by women who are in all other ways equal to men. But if we look more clearly at the current situation, we can see how shaky this illusion of equality really is. To repeat some of the most basic facts: women still do not have the equal political power they have long sought, since only one in five MPs [members of Parliament] is a woman. They do not have economic equality, since the pay gap is still not only large but actually widening. They do not have the freedom from violence they have sought, and with the conviction rate in rape cases standing at just 6 per cent, they know that rapists enjoy an effective impunity in our society.

Rooted in Inequality

There is, of course, nothing intrinsically degrading or miserable about a woman pole-dancing, stripping, having sex with large numbers of partners or consuming pornography. All these behaviours are potentially enjoyable and sexy and fun. But in the current context, in which women's value is so relentlessly bound up with how successfully they are seen as sexually alluring, we can see that certain choices are celebrated, while others are marginalised, and this clearly has a major effect on the behaviour of many women and men.

The hypersexual culture is not only rooted in continuing inequality, it also produces more inequality. When I was talking to [teenager] Carly Whiteley . . . I was struck by her view that a focus on individual choice often ignores the effects of those choices. 'I think the thing is that even if they feel that way for themselves, don't they realise what they are doing for other women?' she said of women who decide to go into stripping or sex work:

> It took us a while to get to where we are now, which is basically where men were at—to be able to insist on respect. And these women are breaking it all down. They are putting us back to where we used to be. Like, if you go to a club now it's not unusual that, say, you'll get your arse slapped by some stranger. Of course you can't complain, you can't say anything—all the media are saying that's OK, all you are is boobs and arse. . . .

Evaluating Appearance, Not Work

If you look at the treatment given to women in political life, you can see how the status of women is now frequently limited by the assumption that they should be judged—often cruelly—on how they measure up to the values not of their work, but of their sexualised appearance. For instance when Ann Widdecombe, the Conservative politician, appeared on the comedy quiz show *Have I Got News For You* in 2007, a large number of the jokes centred on her unsexy looks. The participants quipped about what it would be like to see her pole-dancing, complained that a glance from her would make them lose an erection, and commented freely and nastily on her appearance. Or when Harriet Harman, the deputy leader of the Labour party, commented on the need for more women in power in 2009, one male commentator responded in the *Spectator* magazine, 'So—Harriet Harman, then. Would you? I mean, after a few beers, obviously, not while you were sober . . . I think you wouldn't.' The online version of his article attracted dozens of comments, many along the lines of this one: 'Rod, I wouldn't touch the sanctimonious trollop with yours, let alone mine.'

If a woman in politics does measure up to the right standards of sexiness, that does not make them immune from such bullying. For instance, Sarah Palin, the Republican candidate for the American vice-presidency in 2008, attracted much justified criticism for her political views. Yet nothing justified the torrent of sexual innuendo that she faced at the same time. Manufacturers released a 'naughty schoolgirl' Sarah Palin doll, with a red bra showing through a school uniform blouse, and even a blow-up sex doll. One female commentator in the *Sunday Times* wrote: 'She looks like a porn star, specifically a porn star playing the "good" girl who's about to do something very, very bad. "She's the ultimate MILF ['Mom I'd Like to F--k']," said one friend.' And eventually a porn film was made about a fantasy Palin figure— *Who's Nailin' Palin*? How can young women feel confident about entering public life when they know they are likely to be judged not for their competence and skills, but on how closely they resemble a porn star?

Sexual Bullying Goes Unnoticed

Yet the sexual bullying of women in public life now often goes almost unnoticed, it is so taken for granted. Some of this teasing harks back to a kind of 1950s sniggery nudge-nudge wink-wink, as if the commentators involved were simply amazed to see women, with women's bodies, in public life. For instance, a bizarre furore erupted in 2007 when the then Home Secretary, Jacqui Smith, revealed a little cleavage while speaking in Parliament. It encouraged the *Sun* newspaper to mark a series of female MPs out of ten for the size of their breasts in a feature entitled 'The Best of Breastminster'.

Such bullying feels like an old-fashioned throwback, but this attitude towards women has also been taken up by comedians and performers who see themselves as 'edgy'. When female actors and singers seek publicity by going on chat shows such as Jonathan Ross's on the BBC, they simply have to accept comments about the size of their breasts or how much the host would like to have sex with them. When one writer, India Knight, went to interview the broadcaster Russell Brand, she felt that she was a

How Much Is Beauty Worth?

One full year of tuition and fees at an in-state public college is equal to almost five years of saving $100 a month normally spent on cosmetic beauty products.

One year of tuition and fees is $6,185; five years of beauty products savings is $6,423.

YWCA USA, "Beauty at Any Cost: The Consequences of America's Beauty Obsession on Women and Girls," August 2008, p. 2.

professional doing her normal job. She later tuned into his radio show:

[I was] taken aback to find myself named on air as a prelude to Brand discussing my bosoms with, surreally, Noel Gallagher from Oasis, who insistently asked: "Did you sleep with her?," a question that caused Brand to speculate in some detail about what sleeping with me might have been like . . . it was out of order and reductive: woman, ergo piece of meat, fair game, punchline, nonperson.

Devaluing Other Attributes

This assumption that a woman should be valued primarily for her sexy appearance is having a real effect on women's visibility in our culture. For instance, in sport, it was revealed in 2009 that in the Wimbledon tennis tournament the women selected to play on centre court were being chosen for their looks rather than their tennis rankings. In television in 2009 an older and more experienced woman, Arlene Phillips, was moved aside for a gorgeous but inexperienced young woman, Alesha Dixon, in one of the BBC's flagship family entertainment shows, *Strictly Come Dancing*. In such instances, we can see how a focus on women's physical attributes means that their other attributes, from their sporting prowess to their articulacy to their experience, are devalued. So the equation that is often made between the hypersexual culture and women's empowerment is a false one. Far from being empowering, this culture is claustrophobic and limiting.

This is particularly true of women who may not have other paths towards success and status. The hypersexual culture weighs especially heavily on women with few options in life. For this reason it often seems that the middle classes can dismiss it as being of no relevance to their own lives or the lives of their daughters. It became clear to me that some of the men who create and support this culture do so in the belief that they can protect their own families from its effects. When I talked to some of the powerful people in this industry, I asked them whether they could see their own daughters going into this work. Dave Read, the director of Neon Management, which supplies models to the industry, has a daughter. What would he think if she wanted to be the next Jodie Marsh [a British model and TV personality], I asked, and he was frank. 'I would die to think that she'd try to follow in her footsteps. I want her to have other options.' Phil Edgar-Jones, the creative director of *Big Brother*, also has a young daughter. He started with surprise when I asked how he would feel if she wanted to go into *Big Brother* and do glamour modelling. 'I'm a middle-class parent, so I'd be—' Then he stopped himself. 'If that's what she wanted to do . . . ' He paused again. 'I would hope she would have different aspirations. I encourage her to read books. Other people have different backgrounds.'

Beauty Standards Impact Women Throughout Society

But it is not the case that this change in our culture only affects women in one area or one class. The emphasis on presenting oneself as physically perfect has an impact on women throughout society. When I interviewed girls who were aiming for good degrees and careers I was constantly struck by the way that they were aware of how their boyfriends' expectations of sex would have been formed by pornography and their expectations of women's appearance by the airbrushed standards of current magazine and celebrity culture. These young women returned again and again, despite their academic and creative achievements, to a dissatisfaction with their looks. I have always believed that individuals can enjoy investing time and energy in their looks and clothes without detracting from their freedom, but in our culture this interest in appearance is often more punishing than pleasurable, and tied into an over-vigilant regime of dieting and grooming.

One day I visited a college at Cambridge University, where I talked to five young women who had just received their degree results; more than one had a First [a bachelor's degree], they were looking into bright futures and were full of optimism and excitement. Yet when we talked about body image, it was as though a cloud passed over the sun; smiles dropped, shoulders drooped. 'I really never eat without feeling guilty,' said one, and another agreed. 'From the age of thirteen to seventeen I couldn't put anything in my mouth without worrying,' said another. This kind of punishing attention to their looks may have an effect on women's ability to fulfil their potential in other ways. There has been intriguing research published recently that suggests that women who are put into situations where their attention is directed to their bodies, by the clothes they wear or the advertisements they watch, score worse on maths tests and are less likely to see themselves as decision-makers. Such studies suggest that the narcissism that is being encouraged so relentlessly among young women may be affecting their ability to take up the roles that they would otherwise embrace.

Exalting Market Forces

There has been little questioning of this culture for many years. The tenor of so much of our society has been to exalt the role of the market. If certain magazines sell, if certain clubs make money, if certain images shift products, then dissent about their values is effectively silenced. As Phil Hilton, the ex-editor of *Nuts* [a men's magazine], said to me, 'I've given up on judging people.' So many people would say the same. To judge any aspect of our culture or behaviour is now often seen as impossibly elitist; the market is the only arbiter. Television producers and publishers have told me the same story: that in this society they cannot make decisions based on quality or morality, they must make decisions based on sales. Throughout our society, any attempt to complain about or change this culture is often met by fatalism: if the market is so powerful, then how can any individual stand against it?

To be sure, the current hypersexual culture does not impact equally on all women. There are young women following their dreams in anything from music to literature, campaigning to politics, and throughout their private lives, who have truly benefited from the work done by feminists before them. Yet so many women are hampered by this claustrophobic culture, and feel trapped and frustrated by what is going on around them. Through the glamour-modelling culture, through the mainstreaming of pornography and the new acceptability of the sex industry, through the modishness of lap and pole-dancing, through the sexualisation of young girls, many young women are being surrounded by a culture in which they are all body and only body. In the hypersexual culture the woman who has won is the woman who foregrounds her physical perfection and silences any discomfort she may feel. This objectified woman, so often celebrated as the wife or girlfriend of the heroic male rather than the heroine of her own life, is the living doll who has replaced the liberated woman who should be making her way into the twenty-first century.

| "Never in the history of the world have women had so many amazing opportunities, and it makes not a whit of sense to squander them obsessing over our looks."

Ideals of Beauty Need Not Hinder Women

Raina Kelley

Most women will never meet ever-changing standards of beauty and should ignore them, asserts Raina Kelley in the following viewpoint. Despite claims that attractive women have advantages in the workplace, many opportunities remain for women who do not meet these standards, she maintains. Moreover, Kelley claims, evidence shows that women are making significant gains. Although a professional appearance is valued in the workplace, women should stop worrying about whether beauty standards are unfair and work to increase their market power, which is stronger than the power of beauty, she reasons. Kelley covers society issues and cultural controversies for Newsweek *and the* Daily Beast.

As you read, consider the following questions:
1. Why does Kelley claim she cannot care about the beauty standard?
2. According to an NPD study cited by the author, what does market research reveal about beauty-buying trends?
3. What are some recommendations the author makes for how to deal with concerns about standards of beauty?

Guess what? According to the standard of beauty currently in place in our culture—namely white, young, thin with long, straight hair, I am not beautiful. Can't happen. As a rounded black woman with curly hair, the best I can hope for is moderately attractive. Which means that according to the latest research and *Newsweek*'s own polling, I am at a disadvantage in the workplace, which appears to value looks over education (though not over experience and confidence). But I still don't care about the beauty standards—I don't even care what it is. I can't. For me, it is as immutable and unreachable, and thus as meaningless, as the fact that rich people get better lawyers. So what if the standard is getting stricter, more unrealistic, and meaner by the day? The standard will change, and as bell-bottoms gave way to leg warmers, it'll morph into something else. (Back to foot-binding, perhaps?) And most of us still won't be beautiful by whatever new criteria [fashion designer] Ralph Lauren cooks up. I'll probably never fit into other groups that society favors, either. I'll never be a billionaire. And unless I have a sudden and unprecedented set of surgeries, I'll never be a white man. And yet I somehow managed to graduate from Yale, find a job I sometimes like, and, miracles of miracles, get married and have a kid.

Using Opportunities and Making Strides

Beauty bias notwithstanding, there are still opportunities for people who aren't hotties—lots of them. Virtually all the women

I know have come to terms with the fact that their self-esteem cannot be tied to Photoshopped 15-year-olds on the cover of *Harper's Bazaar*. Never in the history of the world have women had so many amazing opportunities, and it makes not a whit of sense to squander them obsessing over our looks. We do not yet reap rewards equal to those of men. But we can either succeed in the breathtaking arenas that are now open to us—and work to enter more of them—or we can spend our days competing with fashion models and movie stars. In other words, you can be [U.S. Secretary of State] Hillary Clinton or [reality television personality] Heidi Montag. It's your choice.

Despite the $20 billion U.S. beauty industry bearing down on us, and all that media implying that one must look like Gisele [Bündchen, a model] to succeed, girls and women are making extraordinary strides and have done so in a remarkably short period of time. *The Atlantic* just ran a story promising we'd be in charge of the world one day, and the evidence was pretty compelling. We are currently earning the majority of undergraduate (and many graduate) degrees, including medicine and law. We don't have a lot of CEOs [chief executive officers] to call our own, but some of the ones we have, including Carly Fiorina and Meg Whitman [former and current CEO of Hewlett-Packard, respectively], have turned their business prowess into viable political careers. There are a decent number of women in the House and Senate (76 and 17, respectively [as of July 2010], though still low compared with our proportion of the population), but there's no reason that we can't expect those numbers to grow—especially on the heels of Clinton's presidential run and the recent successes of women in the GOP [Republican Party]. Clearly, eligibility for the *Sports Illustrated* swimsuit issue is not required to succeed or even to change the world. And believe it or not, trends in beauty-buying back that up. The market-research firm NPD released a study in April [2010] that revealed that teens and women are now using beauty products in significantly fewer quantities, down 6 percent from 2008 to 2009. Karen Grant, a senior global-industry

Fight "Fatism"

Work on accepting people of all sizes and shapes. . . . It may be useful to create a list of people who you admire that do not have "perfect" bodies; does their appearance affect how you feel about them? It is also important to remember that society's standards have changed significantly over the last 50 years. The women that were considered the "ideal beauties" in the 1940s and 1950s like Marilyn Monroe (size 14) and Mae West were full-bodied and truly beautiful women.

Nicole Hawkins, Hope & Healing,
May 2000.

analyst for NPD, told me its research has shown this is not simply recession-related but that some women are actually becoming less emotionally engaged with the beauty market. Most of the world's women aren't *Vogue*-approved hotties, and still so many manage to kick ass in law school or business school or medical school, and not by sitting in a plastic surgeon's office or the gym all day. Three of the last four secretaries of state have been women—none of whom showed up on the cover of *W.* Sonia Sotomayor may never win a Miss America pageant, but boohoo, she's a Supreme Court justice. I'd choose that over a tiara any day.

Using Economic Power Instead of Looks

I'm not saying you have to completely let yourself go. One of the reasons looks, though not necessarily beauty, are so important to hiring managers is because appearance can help you suss out a lot of information, such as the way you conduct yourself professionally. I suspect if [actress] Angelina Jolie showed up to an interview at an accounting firm in flip-flops and dirty jeans, she'd have trouble getting hired. So despite our fears, looks in the hiring arena do not always equal perfect bone structure. For millennia, beauty was a woman's only currency and, even then, the most gorgeous women were property themselves, unable to inherit land or marry of their own accord. But the days of boobs being our only advantage are as close to being over as they ever have been. We just have to believe it. Stop worrying about unfair beauty standards: 63 percent of Americans are overweight or obese—we need to get healthy, not get liposuction. Getting healthy is the reason I'm on a diet—[model and personality] Tyra Banks has nothing to do it. It's also why I quit smoking. Look around. Most of the world does not look like the Laker Girls or even Coyote Ugly waitresses. And that's OK with them.

And think about it this way. Capitalism always trumps beauty—because it trumps everything. As we continue to grow in power as workers, spenders, heads of households, and legislators, our economic power will force a change in this so-called beauty bias. But we have to be brave and continue to reject the conclusion that turning ourselves into [glamorous actress] Scarlett Johansson is the only way to get ahead. Yes, people can be vicious in their categorization of women's looks. Insult them back or ignore them. It worked for Hillary [Clinton], [former US secretaries of state] Madeleine [Albright], Condoleezza [Rice], and [US Supreme Court justice] Sonia [Sotomayor]. And it looks as though it might just work for [Supreme Court justice] Elena Kagan. Worried you'll never get married because you're not a size zero? Please, 86 percent of American women are married at least once by the age of 40, so stop reading all that lonely-girl porn. Worried that you don't turn heads the way you used to? OK, make a list of everything all that head-turning got you and compare it with what you accomplished when you used your brain instead of a push-up bra. And, I'm sorry, if you are older than 30 and your feelings get hurt by strangers commenting on the thigh sizes of 14-year-olds in a magazine, you need to toughen up. Do something to raise awareness—don't just go looking for a different shade of lipstick. We aren't victims. We aren't objects. And I, for one, am not going to spend my life worrying about when to start Botox treatments. When I'm on my deathbed, I hope to be smiling in satisfaction about all I accomplished, not that I made it to 102 without any cellulite.

> *"Unattractive people are less likely to be hired and promoted, and they earn lower salaries, even in fields in which looks have no obvious relationship to professional duties."*

Discrimination Against Unattractive People in the Workplace Is a Problem

Deborah L. Rhode

In the following viewpoint Deborah L. Rhode argues that workplace discrimination against unattractive people is a serious problem. Indeed, she asserts, studies show that employers are less likely to hire or promote unattractive people, who also earn less money. Although some employers claim that attractiveness can be job-related, several states and local laws reject this argument and ban discrimination based on appearance, Rhode maintains. While proof of discrimination is often difficult to produce, and the stigma of bringing a suit might discourage some, a society that values equal opportunity should oppose all forms of discrimination, she concludes. Rhode, a Stanford University law professor, is author of The Beauty Bias.

As you read, consider the following questions:
1. What example of historically sanctioned discrimination against the unattractive does Rhode cite?
2. According to the author, what did a National Association to Advance Fat Acceptance survey reveal?
3. What did a Cornell University study reveal about the appearance of criminal defendants, as reported by Rhode?

In the 19th century, many American cities banned public appearances by "unsightly" individuals. A Chicago ordinance was typical: "Any person who is diseased, maimed, mutilated, or in any way deformed, so as to be an unsightly or disgusting subject . . . shall not . . . expose himself to public view, under the penalty of a fine of $1 for each offense."

Acceptable Bigotry

Although the government is no longer in the business of enforcing such discrimination, it still allows businesses, schools and other organizations to indulge their own prejudices. Over the past half-century, the United States has expanded protections against discrimination to include race, religion, sex, age, disability and, in a growing number of jurisdictions, sexual orientation. Yet bias based on appearance remains perfectly permissible in all but one state and six cities and counties. Across the rest of the country, looks are the last bastion of acceptable bigotry.

We all know that appearance matters, but the price of prejudice can be steeper than we often assume. In Texas in 1994, an obese woman was rejected for a job as a bus driver when a company doctor assumed she was not up to the task after watching her, in his words, "waddling down the hall." He did not perform any agility tests to determine whether she was, as the company would later claim, unfit to evacuate the bus in the event of an accident.

In New Jersey in 2005, one of the Borgata Hotel Casino's "Borgata babe" cocktail waitresses went from a Size 4 to a Size 6

"You're both so qualified, so I've decided, this only fair way to choose a new secretary - whoever can grab this banana first!"

"You're Both So Qualified, So I've Decided, This Only Fair Way to Choose a New Secretary—Whoever Can Grab This Banana First!," cartoon by M. Moeller. www.CartoonStock.com.

because of a thyroid condition. When the waitress, whose contract required her to keep an "an hourglass figure" that was "height and weight appropriate," requested a larger uniform, she was turned down. "Borgata babes don't go up in size," she was told. (Unless, the waitress noted, they have breast implants, which the casino happily accommodated with paid medical leave and a bigger bustier.)

And in California in 2001, Jennifer Portnick, a 240-pound aerobics instructor, was denied a franchise by Jazzercise, a national fitness chain. Jazzercise explained that its image demanded instructors who are "fit" and "toned." But Portnick was both: She worked out six days a week, taught back-to-back classes and had no shortage of willing students.

Such cases are common. In a survey by the National Association to Advance Fat Acceptance, 62 percent of its overweight female members and 42 percent of its overweight male members said they had been turned down for a job because of their weight.

More than Just Weight

And it isn't just weight that's at issue; it's appearance overall. According to a national poll by the Employment Law Alliance in 2005, 16 percent of workers reported being victims of appearance discrimination more generally—a figure comparable to the percentage who in other surveys say they have experienced sex or race discrimination.

Conventional wisdom holds that beauty is in the eye of the beholder, but most beholders tend to agree on what is beautiful. A number of researchers have independently found that, when people are asked to rate an individual's attractiveness, their responses are quite consistent, even across race, sex, age, class and cultural background. Facial symmetry and unblemished skin are universally admired. Men get a bump for height, women are favored if they have hourglass figures, and racial minorities get points for light skin color, European facial characteristics and conventionally "white" hairstyles.

Yale's Kelly Brownell and Rebecca Puhl and Harvard's Nancy Etcoff have each reviewed hundreds of studies on the impact of appearance. Etcoff finds that unattractive people are less likely than their attractive peers to be viewed as intelligent, likable and good. Brownell and Puhl have documented that overweight individuals consistently suffer disadvantages at school, at work and beyond.

Confirming the Unattractive Bias

Among the key findings of a quarter-century's worth of research: Unattractive people are less likely to be hired and promoted, and they earn lower salaries, even in fields in which looks have no obvious relationship to professional duties. (In one study, economists Jeff Biddle and Daniel Hamermesh estimated that for lawyers, such prejudice can translate to a pay cut of as much as 12 percent.) When researchers ask people to evaluate written essays, the same material receives lower ratings for ideas, style and creativity when an accompanying photograph shows a less attractive author. Good-looking professors get better course evaluations from students; teachers in turn rate good-looking students as more intelligent.

Not even justice is blind. In studies that simulate legal proceedings, unattractive plaintiffs receive lower damage awards. And in a study released this month [May 2010], Stephen Ceci and Justin Gunnell, two researchers at Cornell University, gave students case studies involving real criminal defendants and asked them to come to a verdict and a punishment for each. The students gave unattractive defendants prison sentences that were, on average, 22 months longer than those they gave to attractive defendants.

Reinforcing Stereotypes

Just like racial or gender discrimination, discrimination based on irrelevant physical characteristics reinforces invidious stereotypes and undermines equal-opportunity principles based on merit and performance. And when grooming choices come into play, such bias can also restrict personal freedom.

Consider Nikki Youngblood, a lesbian who in 2001 was denied a photo in her Tampa high school yearbook because she would not pose in a scoop-necked dress. Youngblood was "not a rebellious kid," her lawyer explained. "She simply wanted to appear in her yearbook as herself, not as a fluffed-up stereotype of what school administrators thought she should look like." Furthermore, many grooming codes sexualize the workplace and jeopardize employees' health. The weight restrictions at the Borgata, for example, reportedly contributed to eating disorders among its waitresses.

Appearance-related bias also exacerbates disadvantages based on gender, race, ethnicity, age, sexual orientation and class. Prevailing beauty standards penalize people who lack the time and money to invest in their appearance. And weight discrimination, in particular, imposes special costs on people who live in communities with shortages of healthy food options and exercise facilities.

Looking at Legal Solutions

So why not simply ban discrimination based on appearance?

Employers often argue that attractiveness is job-related; their workers' appearance, they say, can affect the company's image and its profitability. In this way, the Borgata blamed its weight limits on market demands. Customers, according to a spokesperson, like being served by an attractive waitress. The same assumption presumably motivated the L'Oréal executive who was sued for sex discrimination in 2003 after allegedly ordering a store manager to fire a salesperson who was not "hot" enough.

Such practices can violate the law if they disproportionately exclude groups protected by civil rights statutes—hence the sex discrimination suit. Abercrombie & Fitch's notorious efforts to project what it called a "classic American" look led to a race discrimination settlement on behalf of minority job-seekers who said they were turned down for positions on the sales floor. But unless the victims of appearance bias belong to groups already protected by civil rights laws, they have no legal remedy.

As the history of civil rights legislation suggests, customer preferences should not be a defense for prejudice. During the early civil rights era, employers in the South often argued that hiring African Americans would be financially ruinous; white customers, they said, would take their business elsewhere. In rejecting this logic, Congress and the courts recognized that customer preferences often reflect and reinforce precisely the attitudes that society is seeking to eliminate. Over the decades, we've seen that the most effective way of combating prejudice is to deprive people of the option to indulge it.

Similarly, during the 1960s and 1970s, major airlines argued that the male business travelers who dominated their customer ranks preferred attractive female flight attendants. According to the airlines, that made sex a bona fide occupational qualification and exempted them from anti-discrimination requirements. But the courts reasoned that only if sexual allure were the "essence" of a job should employers be allowed to select workers on that basis. Since airplanes were not flying bordellos, it was time to start hiring men.

Answering the Opponents

Opponents of a ban on appearance-based discrimination also warn that it would trivialize other, more serious forms of bias. After all, if the goal is a level playing field, why draw the line at looks? "By the time you've finished preventing discrimination against the ugly, the short, the skinny, the bald, the knobbly-kneed, the flat-chested, and the stupid," Andrew Sullivan wrote in the London *Sunday Times* in 1999, "you're living in a totalitarian state." Yet intelligence and civility are generally related to job performance in a way that appearance isn't.

We also have enough experience with prohibitions on appearance discrimination to challenge opponents' arguments. Already, one state (Michigan) and six local jurisdictions (the District of Columbia; Howard County, Md.; San Francisco; Santa Cruz, Calif; Madison, Wis.; and Urbana, Ill.) have banned such discrimination. Some of these laws date back to the 1970s and 1980s, while some are more recent; some cover height and weight only, while others cover looks broadly; but all make exceptions for reasonable business needs.

Such bans have not produced a barrage of loony litigation or an erosion of support for civil rights remedies generally. These cities and counties each receive between zero and nine complaints a year, while the entire state of Michigan totals about 30, with fewer than one a year ending up in court.

Although the laws are unevenly enforced, they have had a positive effect by publicizing and remedying the worst abuses. Because Portnick, the aerobics instructor turned away by Jazzercise, lived in San Francisco, she was able to bring a claim against the company. After a wave of sympathetic media coverage, Jazzercise changed its policy.

This is not to overstate the power of legal remedies. Given the stigma attached to unattractiveness, few will want to claim that status in public litigation. And in the vast majority of cases, the cost of filing suit and the difficulty of proving discrimination are likely to be prohibitive. But stricter anti-discrimination laws could play a modest role in advancing healthier and more inclusive ideals of attractiveness. At the very least, such laws could reflect our principles of equal opportunity and raise our collective consciousness when we fall short.

| *"For certain jobs, attractiveness is part of the job description."*

Attractiveness Is Necessary for Some Jobs

Mary Elizabeth Williams

Certain jobs require that employees be attractive, maintains Mary Elizabeth Williams in the following viewpoint. Nevertheless, some fashion merchandising companies have come under fire for requiring that their sales associates meet appearance requirements, she claims. While an attractive appearance may not be necessary for jobs outside the public eye, Williams asserts, consumers considering a purchase would prefer a salesperson sporting a look to which they can aspire. Moreover, she reasons, while an attractive appearance is a plus, there is more to success at sales than looks alone. Williams is a staff writer for Salon, *an online magazine of news and commentary.*

As you read, consider the following questions:

1. How did American Apparel respond to claims that its employees must meet an appearance requirement, according to Williams?

2. How does the author compare the appearance requirements associated with her retail and radio station jobs
during college?

3. What does the author say selling products is really about?

It's so disgusting and discriminatory. Have you heard? Retail
clothing companies employing hot people. I just hope the hos-
pitality industry doesn't get wind of this.

Employee-Selection Practices

The fury has been simmering for over a year now, thanks in large
part to the notoriously icky American Apparel [A.A.]. The company, headed by sexual harassment lawsuit magnet Dov Charney,
has always been known for its flesh-flaunting wares and provocative ad campaigns—featuring its own employees and customers.
But after denying last year [in 2009] that it had been systemati-
cally firing staffers who don't pass aesthetic muster, A.A. found
itself at the center of another storm when [website] *Gawker*
pointed out recently its requirement for prospective employees
to submit photos of themselves. "Individuals should be able to
present themselves in a way that impresses and inspires our customers," says American Apparel, while retail experience is "not
necessarily necessary."

A company spokesman elaborated: "We do screen, but not
for beauty. What we look for is personal style." And indeed, a
company unafraid to combine "printed," "Spandex" and "cycle
short" together in one unholy item is a company with unortho-
dox parameters for style. Internal documents reveal an encour-
agement for "full eyebrows," "long, natural hair," no bangs on the
ladies and no goatees on the dudes. Yet despite the company's
insistence that its hiring criteria is a style thing, not a prettiness
thing, the *Gawker* posts brought former and would-be American
Apparel workers out of the woodwork, claiming undue scrutiny
for their allure.

Then on Monday, [August 2, 2010,] *Gawker* busted Abercrombie & Fitch, the retailer long considered the gold standard of softcore homoeroticism, for a similarly looks-ist policy, posting an internal note from the company's now defunct spinoff brand Ruehl. Sample directive: "We must always audit our schedule to assure we have the best looking and best styled associates at all times." Wait—you want people who look good in your clothes to sell them? Oh, the injustice! All the plain people will have to work at Radio Shack!

There are a million reasons to not patronize the likes of American Apparel, a company whose "sweatshop free" philosophy does not exonerate its defiantly ugly wares. That the company would, as it has been accused, base its hiring and promotion practices almost exclusively on looks, that it would blatantly favor employees based on race, is not just messed up, it's flat-out bad business. Good luck running a giant retail chain on the brainpower of 19-year-olds, Dov.

The Role of Appearance in Sales

Yet the contempt for what *Gawker* calls the "breathtakingly superficial" notion that the staff of a store is there to make the merchandise look good seems self-righteously naive. I worked my way through school in various retail gigs and at a radio station— and believe me, the standards for how employees were expected to present themselves in those two milieus could not have been more different. Retail: slender girls who aspired to claw their way to the showroom, who accepted the quid pro quo nature of getting a discount in exchange for swanning around the shop in its wares. Radio: deep-throated shlubby guys.

It's a slippery slope from a store wanting its employees to be part of the customers' aspirational experience to an all-but-stated NO FAT CHICKS policy. And having a sense of style and being beautiful are not the same thing, nor should the latter be the main qualification for a gig that requires long hours, reliability and a knack for working well with the public.

Nevertheless, the fact remains that for certain jobs, attractiveness is part of the job description. Selling anything isn't just about being able to pull a size 9 from the back. It's about being able to make somebody think, "I never thought about how cute that would look belted." It's about making them want to go to the bar where beautiful people pour them drinks. It's peddling the fantasy that given the right socks, you too could be that person/ have that person. Retailers expect a degree of attractiveness from their sales force for the same reasons they put models in their advertisements: to move the merch. Is that unfair? Take it up with the gene pool. If you're my Apple support team, I don't care what you look like. But if you're selling me pants, it's entirely possible that I do.

> "We can't pretend that race isn't a
> major factor in the most harmful of
> beauty ideals."

Media Images of Beauty Hurt Ethnic Women

Lindsay Kite

Although ethnic groups comprise one-third of the US population, women of color are underrepresented in media, maintains Lindsay Kite in the following viewpoint. Unfortunately, she reasons, even when women of color do appear in beauty magazines, editors use Photoshop to lighten their faces and thin their bodies, creating unrealistic ideals. Moreover, studies show that media images have a significant impact on teens' body image; thus the under- and misrepresentation of women of color may explain why second-generation Latinas, for example, have more eating disorders than their mothers do, she suggests. Kite and her sister developed Beauty Redefined, *a healthy body image website.*

As you read, consider the following questions:

1. What did communication scholar Kristen Harrison learn in her survey of African American teen girls?

2. According to Kite, why are for-profit beauty ideals in media working?

3. What evidence does the author provide that women of color in the media must fit white ideals?

In a country where a full one-third of the population is black, Native American, Asian, Pacific Islander, Hispanic or Latina, the serious underrepresentation of women of color in media is really disturbing. Further, when you only account for the women of color shown in positive roles or depictions—especially those depicted as beautiful or desirable—the number is almost negligible. Since *Beauty Redefined* is focused on recognizing and rejecting harmful messages about bodies and beauty in media, we can't pretend that race isn't a major factor in the most harmful of beauty ideals. Images of white women dominate all media—especially roles or depictions featuring "beautiful" or desirable women, not funny sidekicks, the chunky best friend, the hired help or other stereotypes. To think this doesn't have a negative effect on females who rarely see images of their own races depicted in a positive manner is insane. To think it doesn't have an effect on the way white people (and all people) view women of color is equally insane.

What the Studies Show

Since researchers have assumed that black girls were immune to the effects of thin-ideal media, communication scholar Kristen Harrison (2006) conducted a study aimed at testing this idea. Using survey data from 61 African American teen girls, she studied how TV exposure influenced the girls' beliefs about [how] others thought of the girls' own bodies. She discovered that for larger girls, TV exposure significantly influenced their belief that their peers thought they should be smaller. For the smaller girls, TV exposure significantly influenced the belief that their classmates expected them to be larger. In other words, the larger girls in the group assumed their classmates thought they were too fat, while the smaller girls assumed their classmates thought they were too skinny. Interestingly, Harrison found the same result three years earlier when she found white women's exposure to TV beauty ideals predicted the large-busted women wanted smaller chests and small-busted women wanted larger chests.

Basically, that means for-profit beauty ideals in media are *working*. Too many industries thrive off women feeling bad about themselves and seeking ways to fix their "flaws," which women naturally perceive as a result of not measuring up to media standards for beautiful or even "average." These studies (along with plenty of others) show us that pretty much everyone feels bad. Too fat, too thin, too busty, not busty enough, too tall, too white, too dark. . . .

The Whitewashing of Women of Color

The mainstream beauty ideal is almost exclusively white, making it all the more unattainable for women of color. Though beautiful women of color like [American popular culture icons] Beyoncé, Jennifer Lopez, Queen Latifah, Rihanna, Jennifer Hudson, Halle Berry and others have achieved renown in U.S. culture, media representations of these women have become increasingly "anglicized" or "whitewashed" over time, with lighter-colored, straighter hair, lighter makeup, colored contacts and often shrinking figures. Though many of these transformations are likely decided by the celebrities themselves or their styling teams, some of the transformations are much more sinister . . . and more digital. Companies like L'Oréal and Clairol have come under fire for digitally lightening both the skin color and hair color of black women featured in their advertising, including Beyoncé and Queen Latifah. . . .

Even when the women are being recognized for something other than their beauty, like, say, an Oscar nomination for incredibly talented actress Gabourey Sidibe of *Precious*, magazines like

Elle still feel the need to whitewash her in order to feature her image on the cover. While representation of women of color in media has increased slightly over the past decade, finding positive depictions of women with dark skin tones or natural hair is still nearly impossible in mainstream media. Further, when we do see women of color respresented as beauty icons in media, they almost always *already* fit white ideals—meaning they already have light skin tones, light-colored, straight hair, ideally "white" facial features, thin figures, etc. The most famous examples of black or multiracial women celebrated for their beauty or desirability consistently fit those standards, and coming up with examples who don't is really tough. Tyra Banks, Halle Berry, Rihanna, Gabrielle Union, Ciara, Zoe Saldana, Brandy, Janet Jackson, Alicia Keys . . . the list goes on.

For both Latina and black women, research shows beauty ideals include more "feminine curves" than the dominant white ideal. Instead of always subscribing to the thin ideal, girls and women of color, in some cases, value a "thick" ideal, comprising a slender but curvy body, with a thin waist, big breasts and hips and a round behind. Essentially, "the feminine ideal is tanned, healthy slenderness, with no unsightly bumps, bulges, or cellulite, and bodily and facial perfection that results from hours of labor: exercise, makeup, and hair care" [according to researchers R. Coward and A. Kuhn in 1985]—and 25 years later, plastic surgery and digital manipulation.

One recent example of this digital distortion to create (or make women fit) ideals is the notoriously curvaceous actress Sofia Vergara (of the TV show *Modern Family*), whose arm was slimmed to the extreme for Pepsi's "Skinny Can" campaign (barf). Despite a controlling ideal that values "feminine curves" along with the thin ideal, this is still an objectified and unrealistic standard that is a nearly impossible combination for most women, unless extreme photoshopping or expensive and life-threatening cosmetic surgery is performed. Latina and Hispanic girls are still suffering under these controlling standards of beauty.

The Representatives of Black Womanhood Are Light Skinned

Black women are inundated with images of beauty, the faces of which are the likes of Beyoncé, Thandie Newton, Queen Latifah, Halle Berry, [and] Tyra Banks, to name a few. These women are the representative figures of contemporary black womanhood, so we not only see them on beauty magazines and make-up commercials, but in film and television. . . . They all have a similar light-skinned complexion. There appears to be no arena for a dark-skinned woman to shine. . . . The image of the light-skinned black beauty is ubiquitous. Even hip-hop videos overwhelmingly favor the light-skinned vixen.

Cheryl Thompson, Americana, May 2010.
www.americanpopularculture.com.

New Generations Struggle to Resist

In studies where Latina teenage girls report greater body satisfaction compared to white girls, they still report comparable or higher rates of disordered eating. Scary facts: Greater acculturation into mainstream U.S. culture has been associated with preference for much thinner body types among Mexican American women. Studies have found second-generation Mexican Americans had the highest levels of disordered eating among first- through fifth-generation Mexican Americans. In other words, Latinas who are daughters of first-generation Americans were most likely to have an eating disorder, potentially as a result of trying to fit in with U.S. ideals, which may differ starkly from ideas about bodies found in their parents' native cultures. Further, Latina adolescents describe an ideal body type that looks extremely similar to the white norm *and* they report the desire to lose weight at similar rates to their white peers.

Though many studies assume black females are more capable of resisting dangerous thin ideals than white females, plenty of evidence suggests that's simply not true for too many. [R.] Botta found [in a 2000 study] that for both black and white girls, exposure to TV beauty ideals was associated with a stronger drive for thinness and greater body dissatisfaction. [D.F.] Roberts [and U.G. Foehr in 2004] echoed these findings, declaring that black girls may be particularly vulnerable to internalizing media messages that emphasize beauty and appearance. Others have found that the number of hours watching music videos increased the appearance and weight concerns of teen girls, with those findings being strongest among the black girls tested. Generally, television watching is related to lower self esteem and higher levels of disordered eating for girls and young women of all races and ethnicities.

Redefining Beauty

We know different cultures may have different perceptions and definitions of beauty or even thinness, since Asian women considered to be of normal weight and figure in an Asian culture may be considered underweight or anorexic by Westerner ideas of body size. But the central issue here is not so much cultural definitions of beauty or body size—it is the dangerous lengths some people will go in order to achieve those ideals. Essentially, women are viewing a distorted reality and holding themselves to the unattainable standard set by the non reality of popular media—and most often, those standards are based on oppressive, power-laden ideals of whiteness.

Recognizing the ridiculous lack of diversity in representation of media, and particularly when it comes to portrayals of beauty, is absolutely crucial for people of all races. *Recognizing* is the first step toward *rejecting* those messages and the negative feelings they inspire about our bodies. After we reject them, we can continuously *redefine* beauty for ourselves—on our own terms—with the help of the beautiful people in our lives who recognize other forms of beauty as well.

Periodical and Internet Sources Bibliography

The following articles have been selected to supplement the diverse views presented in this chapter.

Jessica Bennett	"The Beauty Advantage," *Newsweek*, July 26, 2010.
Melanie Davis	"The Politics of Office Dress," *The F Word*, October 11, 2011. www.thefword.org.uk.
Elizabeth Dwoskin	"Is This Woman Too Hot to Be a Banker?," *Village Voice*, June 1, 2010.
Economist	"The Line of Beauty: The Economics of Good Looks," August 27, 2011.
Economist	"Ugly Discrimination," August 29, 2011.
Daniel S. Hamermesh	"Ugly? You May Have a Case," *New York Times*, August 27, 2011.
Annette John-Hall	"Plus-Size Image Good and Bad," *Philadelphia Inquirer*, March 2, 2012.
Dahlia Lithwick	"Our Beauty Bias Is Unfair," *Newsweek*, June 14, 2010.
Jeanne B. Martin	"The Development of Ideal Body Image Perceptions in the United States," *Nutrition Today*, May–June 2010.
Minh-Ha T. Pham	"If the Clothes Fit," *Ms.*, Fall 2011.
Giedre Steikunaite	"The Beauty Myth . . . and Madness," *New Internationalist*, March 9, 2011.
Eva Wiseman	"Body Image: More of Us than Ever Hate the Way That We Look. It's Making Us Anxious, Unhealthy and Disempowered," *Observer* (London), June 10, 2012.

CHAPTER 3

Should People Strive for Beauty?

Chapter Preface

"I just wanted to look normal, and now I do,"[1] claims eighteen-year-old Kirsten following breast augmentation surgery—a graduation gift from her parents. Kristen is one of a growing number of teens in the United States electing to have cosmetic surgery. Indeed, in 2010, nearly 219,000 cosmetic surgeries were performed on teens between thirteen and nineteen—a significant increase from 59,890 in 1997. The most common cosmetic surgery performed on teens is octoplasty—the reshaping and/or pinning back of large ears. In 2012, Dr. Thomas Romo, a surgeon from a charity organization that provides free corrective surgery to children born with facial deformities performed octoplasty on fourteen-year-old Nadia Ilse, who had been relentlessly teased since childhood. Some analysts believe that cosmetic surgery is not the solution to bullying or low self-esteem. On the other hand, while most ethical plastic surgeons agree that a fine line exists between corrective and cosmetic surgery, some claim that cosmetic surgery can help teens at risk of destructive behaviors. Whether cosmetic surgery is appropriate for teens is indeed one of several controversies surrounding the question of whether people should strive for beauty.

That Kristen believed breast augmentation would make her appear normal worries those analysts who generally oppose teen cosmetic surgery. They argue that teens are bombarded by images of beauty that are not even real. Indeed, a Dove Self-Esteem Fund survey of a thousand girls between eight and seventeen found that seven in ten of these girls believed that they did not measure up. Indeed, according to Ann Kearney-Cooke, director of the Cincinnati Psychotherapy Institute, "It's clear there is an epidemic of low self-esteem among girls."[2] In fact, Dr. Frederick Lukash, a New York City plastic surgeon told the *New York Times* that "unlike adults who may elect cosmetic surgery for that 'wow' factor to stand out in a crowd, to be rejuvenated and get noticed, kids have a different mantra. They do it to fit in."[3] Kearny-Cooke believes that rather than opt for liposuction, teens with low self-esteem should learn about diet and exercise and to challenge limited definitions of beauty. Like-minded advocates argue that to support cosmetic surgery for teens who are simply unhappy with their bodies sends the message that they are not created right. In fact, New York psychologist Vivian Diller believes that helping children with serious facial deformities due to trauma or those with genetic defects such as cleft palates should be distinguished from "standardizing the heterogeneity that is inherent in being human."[4] She concludes that families and social communities should encourage children to love themselves as they are.

Some commentators claim that blanket condemnation of cosmetic surgery for teens is unfair. While cosmetic surgery among teens has indeed increased, breast augmentation and liposuction, clearly cosmetic and not reconstructive, compose less than 5 percent of cosmetic surgeries performed on teens. These analysts agree that because of reality makeover television shows, some teens may believe that ideal beauty can be achieved with a scalpel. Therefore, argues Michael J. Olding, chief of the Division of Plastic Surgery at the George Washington University School of Medicine, teens "must have sufficient emotional maturity and realistic goals and expectations." While surgeons like Olding agree that cosmetic surgeons must be vigilant when determining whether teens are good cosmetic surgery candidates, "we should not exclude them simply because of their age."[5] Dr. John Canedy, president of the American Society of Plastic Surgeons, agrees. "I'm convinced that there's a group of teen patients that can be helped by cosmetic surgery," he maintains. " The critical thing is to select them thoughtfully and carefully,"[6] Canedy reasons.

Whether cosmetic surgery is appropriate for teens remains hotly contested. While most approve of cosmetic surgery only for those with serious physical deformities, some believe that even purely cosmetic procedures to increase self-esteem are acceptable for teens. The authors in the following chapter present their views in answer to the question, should people strive for beauty? Los Angeles physician Valerie Ulene is optimistic about teen self esteem. "Teenagers naturally begin to feel better about their appearance as they progress through adolescence. Some simply get used to features that they once found bothersome; for others, those features actually change,"[7] she maintains. Unfortunately, some analysts point out, teens are not known for their patience.

Notes

1. Quoted in Camille Sweeney, "Seeking Self-Esteem Through Surgery," *New York Times*, January 15, 2009.
2. Quoted in Sweeney, "Seeking Self-Esteem Through Surgery."
3. Quoted in Sweeney, "Seeking Self Esteem Through Surgery."
4. Vivian Diller, "A Solution to Bullying: Where Do We Draw the Line?," *Huffington Post*, July 31, 2012. www.huffingtonpost.com.
5. Quoted in Jane Friedman, "Cosmetic Surgery," *CQ Researcher*, April 15, 2005.
6. Quoted in Valerie Ulene, "Plastic Surgery for Teens," *Los Angeles Times*, January 12, 2009.
7. Ulene, "Plastic Surgery for Teens."

> *"The more attractive the woman is, the wider her pool of romantic partners and range of opportunities in her work and day-to-day life."*

Striving for Beauty Is Important

Amy Alkon

Claims that women should make no effort to be attractive are naïve, argues Amy Alkon in the following viewpoint. Encouraging women to discount beauty is counterproductive, as appearance does matter when trying to get a job or a mate, she claims. In fact, Alkon asserts, dishonesty about the importance of beauty leads women to extremes that can be embarrassing, frightening, and in some cases unhealthy. The best approach to beauty is to accept that it has some importance but to recognize that character, intelligence, and health are equally valuable, she concludes. Alkon writes a weekly advice column published in numerous newspapers nationwide.

As you read, consider the following questions:

1. What example of affirmative action for ugly people does Alkon provide to satirically support her claim?

2. According to the author, what insulting picture of women does Naomi Wolf paint?

3. In the author's view, why do French women have a more realistic relationship with beauty?

There are certain practical realities of existence that most of us accept. If you want to catch a bear, you don't load the trap with a copy of [novel] *Catch-22*—not unless you rub it with a considerable quantity of raw hamburger. If you want to snag a fish, you can't just slap the water with your hand and yell, "Jump on my hook, already!" Yet, if you're a woman who wants to land a man, there's this notion that you should be able to go around looking like Ernest Borgnine[1]: If you're "beautiful on the inside," that's all that should count. Right. And I should have a flying car and a mansion in Bel Air with servants and a moat.

Welcome to Uglytopia—the world reimagined as a place where it's the content of a woman's character, not her pushup bra, that puts her on the cover of [men's magazine] *Maxim*. It just doesn't seem fair to us that some people come into life with certain advantages—whether it's a movie star chin or a multimillion-dollar shipbuilding inheritance. Maybe we need affirmative action for ugly people; make [actor] George Clooney rotate in some homely women between all his gorgeous girl-friends. While we wish things were different, we'd best accept the ugly reality: No man will turn his head to ogle a woman because she looks like the type to buy a turkey sandwich for a homeless man or read to the blind.

Universal Preferences

There is a vast body of evidence indicating that men and women are biologically and psychologically different, and that what heterosexual men and women want in partners directly cor-responds to these differences. The features men evolved to go for in women—youth, clear skin, a symmetrical face and body, feminine facial features, an hourglass figure—are those indicating that a woman would be a healthy, fertile candidate to pass on a man's genes.

These preferences span borders, cultures, and generations, meaning yes, there really are universal standards of beauty. And while Western women do struggle to be slim, the truth is, women in all cultures eat (or don't) to appeal to "the male gaze." The body size that's idealized in a particular culture appears to correspond to the availability of food. In cultures like ours, where you can't go five miles without passing a 7-Eleven and food is sold by the pallet-load at warehouse grocery stores, thin women are in. In cultures where food is scarce (like in Sahara-adjacent hoods), blubber is beautiful, and women appeal to men by stuffing themselves until they're slim like Jabba the Hutt.

Men's looks matter to heterosexual women only somewhat. Most women prefer men who are taller than they are, with symmetrical features (a sign that a potential partner is healthy and parasite-free). But, women across cultures are intent on finding male partners with high status, power, and access to resources—which means a really short guy can add maybe a foot to his height with a private jet. And, just like women who aren't very attractive, men who make very little money or are chronically out of work tend to have a really hard time finding partners. There is some male grumbling about this. Yet, while feminist journalists deforest North America publishing articles urging women to bow out of the beauty arms race and "Learn to love that woman in the mirror!", nobody gets into the ridiculous position of advising men to "Learn to love that unemployed guy sprawled on the couch!"

Now, before you brand me a traitor to my gender, let me say that I'm all for women having the vote, and I think a woman with a mustache should make the same money as a man with a mustache. But you don't help that woman by advising her, "No need to wax that lip fringe or work off that beer belly!" (Because the road to female empowerment is . . . looking just like a hairy old man?)

The Real Beauty Myth

But take *The Beauty Myth* author Naomi Wolf: She contends that standards of beauty are a plot to keep women politically, economically, and sexually subjugated to men—apparently by keeping them too busy curling their eyelashes to have time for political action and too weak from dieting to stand up for what they want in bed. Wolf and her feminist sob sisters bleat about the horror of women being pushed to conform to "Western standards of beauty" as if eyebrow plucking and getting highlights are the real hardships compared to the walk in the park of footbinding and clitoridectomy [female genital mutilation]. Most insultingly, Wolf paints women who look after their looks as the dim, passive dupes of Madison Avenue and magazine editors. Apparently, women need only open a page of *Vogue* and they're under its spell—they sleepwalk to Sephora [a cosmetics store] to load up on anti-wrinkle potions, then go on harsh diets, eating only carrots fertilized with butterfly poo.

It turns out that the real beauty myth is the damaging one Wolf and other feminists are perpetuating—the absurd notion that it serves women to thumb their noses at standards of beauty. Of course, looks aren't *all* that matter (as I'm lectured by female readers of my newspaper column when I point out that male lust seems to have a weight limit). But looks matter a great deal. The more attractive the woman is, the wider her pool of romantic partners and range of opportunities in her work and day-to-day life. We all know this, and numerous studies confirm it—it's just heresy to say so.

We consider it admirable when people strive to better themselves intellectually; we don't say, "Hey, you weren't born a genius, so why ever bother reading a book?" Why should we treat physical appearance any differently? For example, research shows that men prefer women with full lips, smaller chins, and large eyes—indicators of higher levels of estrogen. Some lucky women have big eyes; others just seem to, thanks to the clever application of eyeshadow. As the classic commercial says, "Maybe she's born with it. Maybe it's Maybelline." (If it increases her options, who cares which it is?)

Dangers of Dishonesty About Beauty

Unfortunately, because Americans are so conflicted and dishonest about the power of beauty, we approach it like novices. At one end of the spectrum are the "Love me as I am!" types, like the woman who asked me why she was having such a terrible time meeting men . . . while dressed in a way that advertised not "I want a boyfriend" but "I'm just the girl to clean out your sewer line!" At the other extreme are women who go around resembling porn-ready painted dolls. Note to the menopausal painted doll: Troweled on makeup doesn't make you look younger; it makes you look like an aging drag queen.

Likewise, being 50 and trying to look 25 through plastic surgery usually succeeds in making a woman look 45 and fembot-scary—an object of pity instead of an object of desire. Plastic surgery you can easily spot is usually a sign—either of really bad work or of somebody who's gone way over the top with it, probably because she's trying to fill some void in her life with silicone, Juvederm, and implanted butt cutlets. There are women who just want to fix that one nagging imperfection. For others, plastic surgery is like potato chips, as in, "Betcha can't eat just one." A woman comes in for a lunchtime lip job—an injection of Restylane or another plumping filler—and ends up getting both sets of lips done. Yes, I'm talking about labiaplasty. (Are *your* vagina lips pouty?)

A Realistic Relationship with Beauty

Once women start seeing wrinkles and crow's feet, the desperation to look like they were born yesterday often makes them act like it, too. Women want to believe there's such a thing as "hope in a jar"—and there is: hope from the CEO [chief executive officer] selling the jars that you and millions of others will buy him a new yacht and a chateau in the south of France. There actually is hope to be found in a plastic bottle—of sunblock, the kind that protects against both UVA and UVB rays (the skin-aging ones). But the Beauty Brains, a group of blogging cosmetic scientists, write, "The sad truth is that creams that claim to be anti-aging are not much more effective than standard moisturizing lotions."

French women, too, buy into the idea that there's some fountain of youth at the Clarins counter. But, perhaps because feminism never seeped into mainstream culture in France like it did here, they generally have a healthier and more realistic relationship with beauty, accepting it as the conduit to love, sex, relationships, and increased opportunities. They take pleasure in cultivating their appearance, and in accentuating their physical differences from men. They don't give up on looking after their looks as they age, nor do they tart themselves up like sexy schoolgirls at 50. They simply take pride in their appearance and try to look like sensual, older women.

To understand what it takes to be beautiful, we need to be very clear about what being beautiful means—being sexually appealing to men. And then instead of snarling that male sexuality is evil, we need to accept that it's just different—far more visually-driven than female sexuality. To focus our efforts, we can turn to an increasing number of studies by evolutionary psychologists on what most men seem to want. For example, the University of Texas' Devendra Singh discovered that men, across cultures, are drawn to a woman with an hourglass figure. Men like to see a woman's waist—even on the larger ladies—so burn those muumuus [shapeless long dresses given to topless Hawaiian women by Christian missionaries in the eighteenth century that became fashionable on the mainland after Hawaii became a state in the 1950s], which only reveal your girlish figure in a Category 5 hurricane, and if you don't have much of a waist, do your best to give yourself one with the cut of your clothes or a belt.

An Honest Approach

Too many women try to get away with a bait-and-switch approach to appearance upkeep. If you spend three hours a day in the gym while you're dating a guy, don't think that you can walk down the aisle and say "I do . . . and, guess what . . . now I don't anymore!" A woman needs to come up with a workable routine for maintaining her looks throughout her lifetime and avoid rationalizing slacking off—while she's seeking a man and after she has one. Yeah, you might have to put five or ten extra minutes into prettying up just to hang around the house. And, sure, you might be more "comfortable" in big sloppy sweats, but how "comfortable" will you be if he leaves you for a woman who cares enough to look hot for him?

Like French women, we, too, need to understand that a healthy approach to beauty is neither pretending it's unnecessary or unimportant nor making it important beyond all else. By being honest about it, we help women make informed decisions about how much effort to put into their appearance—or accept the opportunity costs of going ungroomed. The truth is, like knowledge, beauty is power. So, ladies, read lots of books, develop your mind and your character, exercise the rights the heroes of the women's movement fought for us to have, and strive to become somebody who makes a difference in the world. And, pssst . . . while you're doing all of that, don't forget to wear lipgloss.

Notes

1. Ernest Borgnine was an award-winning actor not known for his physical attractiveness.

"*Studies now document the degree of dissatisfaction women and girls experience with themselves after exposure to unrealistically thin and beautiful female models and actors.*"

The Pursuit of Beauty Is Harmful

Shari Graydon

For many women and girls, exposure to unrealistic standards of beauty leads to poor body image, maintains Shari Graydon in the following viewpoint. In fact, she claims, some become obsessed with their appearance, and others develop eating disorders or resort to dangerous cosmetic surgery. Despite growing concern, she argues, more magazines encourage women to meet increasingly impossible beauty standards, and even celebrities are not immune, as supermarket tabloids cruelly criticize their bodies. Media literacy programs and media activism will help, Graydon reasons, but battling the profitable beauty industry will be a challenge. Graydon, author of In Your Face: The Culture of Beauty and You, *is a writer and media consultant.*

Shari Graydon, "How the Media Keeps Us Hung Up on Body Image," *Herizons*, Summer 2008, vol. 22, no. 1, p. 16. Copyright © 2008 by Herizons. All rights reserved. Reproduced by permission.

As you read, consider the following questions:

1. To what type of power does Graydon compare the make-over industry culture?
2. How have the tabloids responded to young stars such as Lindsay Lohan, Nicole Richie, and Kate Olsen?
3. According to the author, why is it impossible to deny the reach of media images?

The rap sheet gets longer every year—spend five minutes in the slow line at your local supermarket checkout and you can't avoid being reminded of the heinous nature of crimes against women's body image. "[Actor and recording artist] Janet Jackson's shocking weight gain!" scream the headlines; "[Actor] Jennifer Love-Hewitt's butt is enormous!" and "[Recording artist and celebrity Victoria Beckham aka] Posh has dimpled legs!"

Fortunately, help is at hand, often within the very same publications. Not coincidentally, they promise "Foods that erase belly fat!" and "Professional trainer's tips to get bikini-ready!"

The Makeover Industry

After decades of feminist activism and enlightenment, how is it we're still here? Strange, but true, the cautionary words of Dwight Eisenhower provide an instructive parallel. In 1960, with a perceptiveness that eluded him in office, the outgoing U.S. president warned, "we must guard against the acquisition of unwarranted influence, whether sought or unsought, by the military-industrial complex."

Substitute "makeover-industry culture" for "military industrial complex" and you get the same "disastrous rise of misplaced power" Eisenhower cautioned against. And, just as America's dedication of resources to military operations has grown significantly in recent decades, so has there been a veritable explosion in the number of commercial enterprises with a vested financial interest in ensuring that women and girls are more at war with their bodies than ever before.

Consider that in 2008 the legion of aggressively promoted makeover solutions to remedy our failure to live up to feminine ideals has gone far beyond mere cosmetics, exercise regimes and diet programs. The fixes now on offer include liposuction, stomach stapling, anti-cellulite creams, breast, butt, cheek and chin implants, Botox and collagen injections, chemical peels, facelifts and labia surgery.

The list is heart-stopping—sometimes literally. At least three prominent women have died in recent years from complications from plastic surgery: Olivia Goldsmith, the American fiction writer who penned *The First Wives Club*; Micheline Charest, a prominent Quebec communications executive; and Donda West, the mother of popular hip hop artist Kanye West. No doubt others have, too. They just haven't made headlines, because without the celebrity connection the news would be merely tragic, as opposed to titillating.

Given the advent of size-zero fashions, and, with television series such as *Extreme Makeover* and *The Swan* promoting surgery as a means of achieving the impossible, such deaths aren't surprising. But when even the teenagers and twenty-somethings actually blessed with skinny genes are collapsing from starvation on fashion runways, the damage being caused by the cultural normalization of "extreme" is undeniable.

Belated and Disingenuous Responses

In search of a contemporary trend to feel good about, it was tempting last year [2007] to celebrate the fact that fashion shows in Milan and Madrid imposed a minimum body mass index [BMI] (height/weight fat ratio) on the female models they hired. The British Fashion Council declined to establish a minimum BMI, but announced that it recognized its "responsibility" and had asked its designers to use only "healthy" models aged 16 or older.

Unfortunately, all these industry responses were belated re-actions to the public outrage that greeted two highly publicized deaths. In August 2006, Uruguayan model Luisel Ramos starved herself for her career and was rewarded with heart failure that killed her at the age of 22. Three months later, her 21-year-old Brazilian colleague Ana Carolina Reston also died of complica-tions resulting from anorexia.

The French have always claimed one must suffer to be beau-tiful, but you're forgiven for believing that obscenely premature death may actually defeat the purpose. Insisting that models conform to a minimum body mass index is also not a progres-sive solution.

Merryl Bear, director of [Canada's] National Eating Disorder Information Centre, calls the move "completely disingenuous. The fashion industry has downloaded responsibility to the very people who have the least power," she says. "Models are at the bottom of the food chain."

At the top are the designers, photographers and editors who continue to deny the political context altogether, maintaining that their preferred slim physiques are merely an aesthetic choice, fuelled by the perception that clothes drape better on bodies that resemble wire coat hangers.

A Deluge of Unrealistic Images

Unfortunately, that aesthetic has helped to drive a multibillion-dollar industry that thrives by distracting women away from a focus on what our bodies do, overwhelming us instead with im-ages of how they ought to look. The result is that, compared to our sisters of a generation ago, women today have an unprec-edented number of opportunities to judge themselves against a select and genetically freakish few.

It's true that [1960s English model] Twiggy inspired some serious dieting behaviour in her day. But the iconic waif was nei-ther ubiquitous nor replicated by dozens of high-profile imita-tors. Today, in contrast, stars like Lindsay Lohan, Nicole Ritchie,

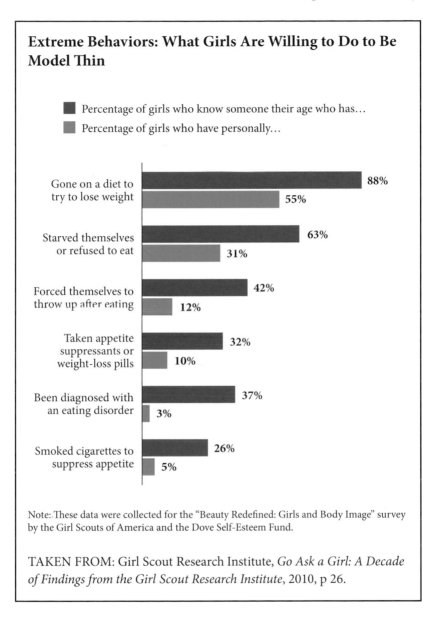

Extreme Behaviors: What Girls Are Willing to Do to Be Model Thin

■ Percentage of girls who know someone their age who has…

■ Percentage of girls who have personally…

Gone on a diet to try to lose weight — 88% / 55%

Starved themselves or refused to eat — 63% / 31%

Forced themselves to throw up after eating — 42% / 12%

Taken appetite suppressants or weight-loss pills — 32% / 10%

Been diagnosed with an eating disorder — 37% / 3%

Smoked cigarettes to suppress appetite — 26% / 5%

Note: These data were collected for the "Beauty Redefined: Girls and Body Image" survey by the Girl Scouts of America and the Dove Self-Esteem Fund.

TAKEN FROM: Girl Scout Research Institute, *Go Ask a Girl: A Decade of Findings from the Girl Scout Research Institute*, 2010, p 26.

Paris Hilton, Misha Barton and Kate Olsen are regularly celebrated and condemned alike for what, in a neonatal ward, would be termed "failure to thrive." In fact, the voracious tabloids have ensured that their performances on the consumption stage (eat normally or walk the red carpet with pride—you decide) have largely eclipsed whatever artistic talents originally made them famous.

Yesteryear's magazine racks sported exponentially fewer publications devoted to fame voyeurism and advising women on the finer points of dressing up, dressing down or sculpting our bodies in pursuit of a profile that we'd be happy to avoid dressing altogether. *Cosmo[politan]* and *Vogue* are now buried under a deluge of other fashion and "fitness" magazines, while a host of new titles supplement the print lessons available to male readers regarding what's "desirable" and "ideal" when it comes to the sizes and shapes of women's body parts.

Furthermore, the body parts on display have become less and less realistic. In addition to the ubiquitous presence of breast implants, increasingly sophisticated Photoshop technology now permits an unprecedented degree of artificiality in application to hips, thighs, waists, arms and necks. We are reminded of this only occasionally, when someone like [actor] Kate Winslett has the temerity to question the aggressive airbrushing that some magazine has used to transform her body into an unrecognizable mannequin.

Meanwhile, models themselves are becoming smaller, even as real women grow larger. Analyses of the body sizes of *Playboy* centrefolds and Miss America contestants over the years have demonstrated diminishing trends in both cases. Pageant winners have become significantly slimmer and less curvaceous, and almost all of the contemporary centrefolds assessed in a 1999 study were considered underweight in the context of Canadian guidelines. Close to a third met the World Health Organization's BMI criteria for anorexia.

The Impact of Distorted Images

It may be small consolation to know that our depth of understanding about the impact of these images on our emotional, psychological and physical health has improved. Dozens of peer-reviewed academic studies now document the degree of dissatisfaction women and girls experience with themselves after exposure to unrealistically thin and beautiful female models and actors. Indeed, the more time we spend immersed in contemporary media, the more likely we are to obsess about our appearance or develop disordered eating behaviour.

Quantifying the incidence of eating disorders remains a challenge, says Bear, in part because of differing definitions and the dependency of researchers on self-identification. Some studies suggest that the rates of anorexia stabilized in the 1980s, while those of bulimia continue to increase. The affected population is also changing: Many women in midlife who previously had no history of disordered eating now appear to be developing problems.

Media images are never a sufficient condition, of course; many other factors contribute. But it's impossible to deny their reach. Recent research published in the *Canadian Medical Association Journal* found that close to one in three preadolescent girls is trying to lose weight and one in 10 shows symptoms of an eating disorder.

Among younger women and girls, says Bear, eating disorders have the highest mortality rates of all psychiatric disorders. Girls affected are 12 times more likely to die than those who are not, she says, and disordered eating has become the third most chronic illness in adolescence.

Nor should we be encouraged by the migration of young media consumers away from print and TV sources and onto the Internet. The vast storehouses of pornography available on the Net reinforce equally distorted visions, not just of women's bodies but of how they "desire" to be "used." And so far the self-posted images of a new generation of young women who use social networking sites to become media creators as well as consumers suggest the commercial landscape's dominant trends are being replicated more often than they're challenged.

What can we do in response?

On a macro scale, the challenge is as fraught today as it ever was. We're up against individual plastic surgeons and multinational corporations alike, all of whom have a vested interest in continuing to feed the commodification of insecurity. Even the makers of Dove, which won the customer loyalty of millions of women for using images of diverse non-models, remains part of the problem. (Reflecting the cynical self-interest of the industry at large, its parent company Unilever also markets products like SlimFast and Fair and Lovely, a skin-whitening agent.)

Alternative Media and Media Literacy

And yet the explosion of alternative media sources—this magazine [*Herizons*] among them—does give us some options. In 2008, it is possible for individuals to avoid mainstream magazines and TV shows that perpetuate body image trauma while offering news and entertainment. In the process of supporting feminist media producers and promoting the analysis found there, we can also shore up our own resistance to the images' impact when we are exposed.

Media literacy programs in schools provide similar protection for young people. Teaching critical thinking in application to how media industries work—how media images are constructed and why—nurtures kids' skepticism and gives them some capacity to challenge the implicit and explicit claims made.

Changing the pictures themselves is much more difficult. We can hope the resonance achieved by the Dove campaign signals that the pendulum has swung as far into artifice as it can and is now poised to drift back into the authenticity zone. Or we can help it along by mobilizing our networks to deliver messages about consumer dissatisfaction to the people and companies responsible for the creation and dissemination of unhealthy, destructive images.

We know this is important, though few of us actually take the time to do it. But as MediaWatch discovered in the 1990s, it's actually not enough to boycott retrograde companies or even to enroll our friends in joining the fight. We actually have to let the manufacturers, advertisers, publishers and programmers know that they're losing business by behaving in unethical and destructive ways. In the process, we might inform them of recent British research finding that skinny models aren't any more effective at selling products than regular-sized women, and encourage them to capitalize on the real-women trend spearheaded by Dove.

The tactics may seem laughably inadequate to the task of toppling the mammoth makeover industry culture, but at very least, by engaging in such manoeuvres, we'll be directing our firepower at the real enemy, and away from our own perfect reflections in the mirror.

"A surgeon performing African American rhinoplasty . . . can work to enhance ethnic features, as opposed to changing them to fit inappropriate standards of beauty."

In a Landmark Paper Just Published in the Prestigious *Archives of Facial Plastic Surgery*, an Innovative Technique in African American Rhinoplasty Proves to Preserve Ethnicity, Increase Self-Esteem

Biotech Week

In the following viewpoint, Biotech Week profiles the techniques of Dr. Oleh Slupchynskyj. Dr. Slupchynskyj uses a three-tiered surgical approach that preserves ethnic characteristics of African American patients when they receive rhinoplasty. In the past, rhi-

noplasty had been used to create a more Caucasian look. But with his technique, Slupchynskyj preserves ethnic characteristics, improving his patients' satisfaction and overall self-esteem. Biotech Week *is a magazine for the biotechnology and pharmaceutical industries published by NewsRX.*

As you read, consider the following questions:

1. What is the most common cosmetic procedure in the African American population, according to the article?
2. Who is Oleh Slupchynskyj?
3. How many African Americans participated in the study?

In a groundbreaking study involving 75 African American patients, Dr. Oleh Slupchynskyj, Founder and Director of The Aesthetic Facial Surgery Institute of New York and New Jersey, statistically proves a unique three-tiered surgical approach in rhinoplasty results in an excellent degree of preservation of ethnic characteristics, very high patient satisfaction postoperatively and consistently increased self-esteem.

The nose is the central feature of the face; therefore it can easily enhance or detract from one's overall facial aesthetics. In its 2005 survey, the American Academy of Facial Plastic and Reconstructive Surgery found that rhinoplasty was the most common cosmetic procedure in the African American population averaging at 65%. "Rhinoplasty, a procedure that was sometimes used in an attempt to make an African American nose look more Caucasian, has evolved a great deal as societal understanding of ethnic beauty and surgical techniques for ethnic features have improved," Dr. Slupchynskyj reports. "A surgeon performing African American rhinoplasty should be aware of, and be able to distinguish, the various standards of beauty present in different ethnic groups; only then s/he can work to enhance ethnic features, as opposed to changing them to fit inappropriate standards of beauty."

In this study, all 75 African American patients sought: 1) nasal dorsal augmentation for inadequate nasal dorsal height; 2) elevation of a low or depressed nasal-frontal angle; 3) refinement of a poorly defined, rounded or bulbous nasal tip; 4) reduction of nasal width both horizontally and vertically. To address these common issues the three-tiered approach to African American rhinoplasty was used in all 75, and Dr. Slupchynskyj found it to be a technique that yields great patient satisfaction, allows for maintenance of ethnic features, and yields a minimal rate of complications. This three-tiered approach enhances the equilibrium of the nose and face by increasing dorsal height, lessens nasal flare, and increases tip refinement and projection, while maintaining ethnic characteristics. "According to the results of our study, the majority of patients indicated a low, if any, change in ethnic characteristics," said Dr. Slupchynskyj. Concurrently, when addressing patient satisfaction with the result of this technique, an overwhelming number of patients indicated average or above-average satisfaction with their result. Finally, Dr. Slupchynskyj states, "When the high increase in self-esteem due to this procedure is considered with our study results, we can indicate this technique as one that successfully addresses concerns of African American patients seeking rhinoplasty surgery. African American patients are not looking to change their ethnic features; they seek satisfaction from a nose that is in harmony with the remainder of their facial features."

The *Archives of Facial Plastic Surgery* is the official publication for the American Academy of Facial Plastic and Reconstructive Surgery, Inc., the European Academy of Facial Plastic Surgery, and the International Federation of Facial Plastic Surgery Societies.

Oleh Slupchynskyj, M.D. is the director and founder of the Aesthetic Facial Surgery Institute of New York and New Jersey with offices in Manhattan and West Orange and has been in private practice for over 10 years. Born and raised in Manhattan, Dr. Slupchynskyj is double board certified through the American

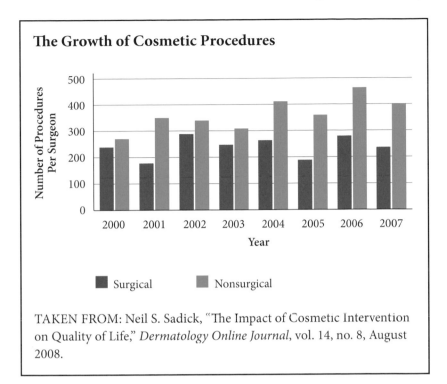

The Growth of Cosmetic Procedures

TAKEN FROM: Neil S. Sadick, "The Impact of Cosmetic Intervention on Quality of Life," *Dermatology Online Journal*, vol. 14, no. 8, August 2008.

Board of Facial Plastic Surgery and the American Board of Otolaryngology with training specific to the head, neck and face. He is named one of the top plastic surgeons of 2007 by the Consumers' Research Council of America and is considered a face specialist. His SLUPLift mini-lift was recently featured on CBS2 News. He has also been featured on NY1 News, the *New York Daily News*, *Vogue*, *Woman's World*, *Gotham*, *Redbook*, *Jane* and *Time Out NY*. He is a member of the following Societies: American Academy of Facial Plastic and Reconstructive Surgery, American Academy of Otolaryngology, New York County Medical Society, American Academy of Otolaryngic Allergy and American Academy of Cosmetic Surgery. More information on his surgical techniques can be found on the websites www .facechange.org and www.africanamericanrhinoplasty.com.

> "Some patients may overlook the
> risks of aesthetic surgery because it is
> performed by doctors."

The Risks of Cosmetic Surgery Should Not Be Ignored

Alexander Edmonds

Because cosmetic surgery is performed by doctors, some patients may ignore the risks, maintains Alexander Edmonds in the following viewpoint. People generally weigh the risk of a surgical procedure against the potential health improvement, he claims; however, since nonreconstructive cosmetic procedures are not necessary, calculating the risk is difficult, Edmonds claims. Moreover, he argues, the ethics of performing surgery that can cause harm without curing or preventing a disease make cosmetic surgery itself questionable. Nevertheless, he reasons, because aesthetic surgeries have become established, doctors must make patients aware of the dangers. Edmonds, a professor of anthropology at the University of Amsterdam, is the author of Pretty Modern: Beauty, Sex and Plastic Surgery in Brazil.

As you read, consider the following questions:

1. What evidence does Edmonds provide that there has been a surprising lack of agreement about the safety of Poly Implant Prothèse breast implants?

2. Why did nineteenth-century plastic surgeons limit themselves to reconstructive procedures, in the author's opinion?

3. What examples does the author give of his claims that cosmetic surgeries lie in a gray zone between necessity and medical enhancement?

The faulty breast implants made by the French company Poly Implant Prothèse, or PIP, have grabbed headlines around the world in recent weeks [January 2012], and it's no wonder. The prostheses are more prone to rupture than other models, and they contain an industrial grade of silicone never intended for use in a medical device. The scandal is also global in scope. Sold in 65 countries, the implants were re-branded by a Dutch company registered in Cyprus, offered on credit in Venezuela and smuggled into Bolivia, where they were bought by medical tourists.

There has been a surprising lack of agreement about the safety of the implants. In France, women were advised to have them removed—at public expense. But British health officials blandly stated there was a "lack of evidence" linking PIP implants to cancer.

That some 300,000 women around the world received the implants seems at first glance to be a spectacular example of medical malfeasance and regulatory ineptitude. But the scandal also raises a more basic question: Are the risks of any aesthetic surgery acceptable?

The Challenge of Calculating Risk

Calculating health risks is especially difficult with aesthetic procedures. With most surgeries, the risks are weighed against expected health improvements. But aesthetic procedures, by definition, do not improve health. For this reason, 19th century plastic surgeons limited themselves to reconstructive procedures in a bid for medical acceptance. Today, cosmetic plastic surgeries outnumber reconstructive ones in many countries. Yet the same ethical concerns that early plastic surgeons had with performing aesthetic procedures have never been resolved.

Some patients may overlook the risks of aesthetic surgery because it is performed by doctors. The ritual elements of medicine—the white coats, the bedside manner—powerfully symbolize health. The fact that a surgeon is putting in implants sends a subtle message that they are safe. What healer would do something to harm us?

One response to the PIP scandal would be a ban on doctors performing cosmetic breast augmentation altogether. It's well known that breast implants of many types can cause burning pain, loss of sensation, hardening of breast tissue and serious infection. One woman who suffered complications from implants has filed a petition with the Scottish government urging adoption of such a ban. An argument could even be made that aesthetic surgery violates the Hippocratic oath [taken by medical doctors] because it carries a potential for harm without curing or preventing disease.

But banning cosmetic surgeries would be difficult to enforce internationally. More than half a million U.S. residents went abroad last year [2011] for medical care, and elective treatments such as cosmetic surgery are the most popular treatments. Though the PIP implants were not authorized for use in the United States, they were sold to American medical tourists in countries such as Brazil.

Defining What Is Cosmetic

More important, aesthetic surgeries and procedures have become an established part of medical practice. They are no longer just the domain of plastic surgeons and dermatologists but are increasingly performed by GPs [general practitioners], OB-GYNs [obstetricians and gynecologists], endocrinologists and other medical specialists, a trend known as "practice drift." And

Teenage Surgical Procedures, 2011

Surgical Procedure	# of Procedures Performed in 2011	% change from 2010
Laser hair removal	69,434	4%
Nose reshaping	33,892	-3%
Laser skin resurfacing	23,590	21%
Laser treatment of leg veins	21,882	9%
Breast reduction in men	14,371	6%
Ear surgery	7,489	-15%
Liposuction	3,248	1%
Hyaluronic acid	3,248	14%
Chin augmentation	1,809	69%

Note: These figures represent the total number of each procedure performed in 2011 and the percent change from 2010 for thirteen- to nineteen-year-olds. Statistics are from the American Society of Plastic Surgeons.

TAKEN FROM: Simon Rogers, "US Plastic Surgery Statistics: Chins, Buttocks and Breasts Up, Ears Down," *Guardian* [UK], April 19, 2012.

the sheer availability of a procedure can make it appear necessary. Cosmetic dentistry is so common it is not always thought of as "cosmetic"—and woe to the American parent who begrudges it to a child.

Some plastic surgeries similarly lie in a gray zone between necessity and medical enhancement. For example, breast reduction is seen by many in the United States as medically justifiable. But in Brazil the operation often has mainly a cosmetic aim (small breasts are an erotic ideal, while larger breasts are seen as matronly). Reconstructive surgeries such as breast implants following a mastectomy also concern aesthetics. As with cosmetic augmentation, the goal is not to improve function but appearance. Of course, breast cancer patients are usually seen as medically entitled to implants, which, not surprisingly, are often available for free.

Still, classifying breast implants as reconstructive does not mean they are less risky. At least a fifth of the French women with PIP implants received them after mastectomies. Calculating risks with any form of plastic surgery is difficult because it depends on weighing potential harm to the body against improvements to intangible qualities such as sexual and psychological well-being.

Perhaps the latest implant scandal is just a misstep on the path to greater safety in aesthetic surgeries. In 2006, the FDA [Food and Drug Administration] ended a 14-year moratorium on silicone implants with the approval of two new models. Shortly after, breast augmentation became the most commonly performed cosmetic surgery in the U.S.

But while medical advances can result in safer cosmetic procedures, they can also contribute to their normalization. Yesterday's vanity is often today's health, or at least well-being. As beauty becomes a more visible part of medicine, health risks may become less visible. And that is a big risk.

Periodical and Internet Sources Bibliography

The following articles have been selected to supplement the diverse views presented in this chapter.

Dominique Browning	"The Case for Laugh Lines," *New York Times*, May 29, 2011.
Denise Campbell	"Dying for the Promise of Perfection," *Black Enterprise*, June 2009.
Environmental Defence (Canada)	"Heavy Metal Hazard: The Health Risks of Hidden Heavy Metals in Face Makeup," May 2011. http://environmentaldefence.ca.
James S. Fell	"Vanity Can Be Healthy Asset," *Los Angeles Times*, August 20, 2011.
Donna Henderson-King and Kelly D. Brooks	"Materialism, Sociocultural Appearance Messages, and Paternal Attitudes Predict College Women's Attitudes About Cosmetic Surgery," *Psychology of Women Quarterly*, vol. 33, 2009.
Jane Houlihan	"Why This Matters—Cosmetics and Your Health," Environmental Working Group, April 13, 2011. www.ewg.org/skindeep.
Caitlin Kenny	"Your Views on Beauty," *Flare*, September 2011.
Amy Muise and Serge Desmarais	"Women's Perceptions and Use of 'Anti-aging' Products," *Sex Roles*, vol. 63, 2010.
Observer	"Cosmetic Surgery: Out of a Scandal Must Come Proper Regulation," January 8, 2012.
Autumn Whitefield-Madrano	"Living with Contradiction: Beauty Work and Feminism," *Feministe*, August 1, 2011.

What Are the Societal Effects of the Beauty and Fashion Industries?

Chapter Preface

In 1997, a fifteen-year-old girl named Caty asked to meet with Adi Barkan, a prominent Israeli photographer and fashion model agent. She wanted to learn what a model should look like. When she arrived, Caty stood five-foot-seven-inches tall and weighed seventy-nine pounds. Barkan immediately recognized that she required hospitalization. During the next five months, he visited her daily. He became committed to understanding the world of anorexics and bulimics. According to Barkan, the fashion world responded to his efforts to deal with the issue of model health with disdain, apathy, and even insults. Thus, Barkan concluded, "only legislation can change the situation."[1] Indeed, with the help of Israeli parliament member Rachel Adato, Barkan championed a law that passed on March 19, 2012. The bill required that the fashion and advertising industry ban underweight models as determined by body mass index (BMI), an index of the ratio of a person's weight to his or her height. The regulations were not only concerned with unhealthy models but also the impact of unrealistic images in advertising. Thus, the law also regulated the use of Photoshop (an image-altering software program) in advertising. The Israeli regulations gained media attention worldwide. US commentators noted that in the United States such regulations would raise the question of how to balance the First Amendment right to freedom of speech against the need to protect the well-being of consumers. Indeed, one of several controversies in the debate concerning the effects of the beauty and fashion industries is whether or not they should be regulated.

Some analysts argue that while unrealistic images of beauty in fashion advertising may not cause eating disorders, they are a contributing factor. Daniel Le Grange, psychiatry professor and director of the eating disorder program at the University of Chicago, asserts, "No one is that perfect, no one has Photoshop on their faces all day long." While he acknowledges that eating disorders are complex diseases in which genetic, environmental, and societal factors combined make some individuals more vulnerable than others, he claims legislation like the Israeli laws can protect vulnerable people from environmental factors. "It's very discouraging for our patients who for one reason or another desire that perfection, and they page through every magazine and see every face that's perfect. It's easy to get scooped up in that, 'I should look perfect because they all look perfect.'"[2] However, in the United States such laws would face strict scrutiny.

Laws that require the fashion industry to monitor the body weight of fashion models and that regulate images in magazines would require that the harm to the public be unambiguous. Unfortunately, the impact of media images on eating disorders is unclear, as Le Grange concedes. According to University of Wisconsin professor and First Amendment expert Donald Downs, a law such as that enacted in Israel "would be in tension with American cultural support for free speech in cases in which the harm is not direct or clear."[3] The approach in the United States is to put public pressures on industries to change.

Indeed, the Council for Fashion Designers of America (CFDA) in 2007 formed a health initiative that it says "is about awareness and education, not policing."[4] However, it failed to require that models get a doctor's physical examination to assess their health and BMI. In the eyes of some, this reflects a failure of the fashion industry to protect their employees from within. Photographers who support the use of Photoshop argue that fashion photography has always been manipulated. Indeed, legs were lengthened with a wide angle lens and skin smoothed through overexposure. However, critics argue that these procedures were costly and time consuming and thus rarely used. According to Jenna Sauers on the feminist website Jezebel, "What used to be a one-shot procedure can now be reverted, re-attempted, undone, re-done, and tweaked again and again as necessary. Never before have images been so highly malleable, so easily 'perfectable.'

What used to be exceptional and difficult has now been made easy—and it's become the norm."[5]

Whether Congress should enact a law similar to that passed in Israel thus remains controversial. Central to this debate is the impact of the beauty and fashion industries. Indeed, the authors in the following chapter present their views in answer to the question, what are the societal effects of the beauty and fashion industries? In 2012, eighth-grader Julia Bluhm gathered more than eighty thousand signatures on a petition asking *Seventeen* magazine to stop digitally altering body sizes or face sizes on its editorial pages. In a National Public Radio interview, she advises, "If you're looking for a girlfriend who looks like the models that you see in magazines, you're never going to find a girlfriend, because those people are edited with computers."[6] The staff of *Seventeen* did, in fact, sign an eight-point Body Peace Treaty, evidence that some in the fashion media recognize the public's interest in a need for change.

Notes

1. Quoted in Talya Minsberg, "What the U.S. Can—and Can't—Learn from Israel's Ban on Ultra-Thin Models," *Atlantic*, May 2012.
2. Quoted in Minsberg, "What the U.S. Can—and Can't—Learn from Israel's Ban on Ultra-Thin Models."
3. Quoted in Minsberg, "What the U.S. Can—and Can't—Learn from Israel's Ban on Ultra-Thin Models."
4. Council of Fashion Designers of America, CFDA Health Initiative, January 12, 2007. http://cfda.com.
5. Jenna Sauers, "Regulating Photoshop: A Hazy Proposition, Not a Solution," *Jezebel*, July 26, 2010. http://jezebel.com.
6. Quoted in Elise Hu, "*Seventeen* Magazine Takes No-Photoshop Pledge After 8th-Grader's Campaign," *Two-Way* (blog), July 5, 2012. www.npr.org.

"Alterations made through processes like Photoshop can contribute to unrealistic body image expectations."

Altered Fashion Magazine Photographs Contribute to Unrealistic Body Images

Vivian Diller

In the following viewpoint Vivian Diller asserts that the American Medical Association's stand against manipulative advertising, such as using Photoshop to create distorted images of models and celebrities, reflects concern about the impact of unrealistic images on teen health. People need to relieve America's youth of the pressure to meet unrealistic body standards established by distorted images, she claims. According to Diller, organizations promoting teen health do not want to ban Photoshop but to establish some guidelines for those who create images that impact teens. Diller, a psychologist, is coauthor with Jill Muir-Sukenick of Face It: What Women Really Feel as Their Looks Change.

As you read, consider the following questions:

1. According to Diller, how did Kate Winslet and Brad Pitt express their concern that Photoshop had gone too far?

2. What dramatic policy was suggested by French parliament member, Valerie Boyer, as reported by the author?

3. What are some of the debatable issues that remain about Photoshop, in the author's view?

Has Photoshop gone too far? Kate Winslet and Brad Pitt are among several public figures who think so and the American Medical Association (AMA) is now backing them up.

Taking a Stand

Winslet was one of the first to break ground when she took action against *GQ* magazine for digitally altering her body in its photographs—making her unrealistically thin. Pitt requested that there be no retouching on his *W* magazine cover, personally selecting Chuck Close to shoot it, a photographer known for his extremely detailed portraits that expose skin flaws. While most people dream of magically removing their pounds and wrinkles—and some celebs demand it—more and more are seeing Photoshop as dangerous terrain.

The American Medical Association (AMA) recently announced it was taking a stand against image manipulation in advertising, stating that alterations made through processes like Photoshop can contribute to unrealistic body image expectations, eating disorders and other emotional problems. Surprisingly, professional and public reactions are mixed.

One eating disorder specialist, Carrie Arnold, reacted with "show me the evidence." In her piece, "What's Photoshop Got to Do with It?," she quotes the AMA as saying "a large body of literature" exists linking media exposure to eating disorders, but after Arnold did her research, she found little scientific evidence to support the statement. The studies AMA cited just don't connect Photoshop to diagnosable eating disorders, as spelled out by the DSM-IV.[1] She writes, "We don't think ads for disinfectant somehow promote OCD [obsessive-compulsive disorder]. We also don't think that those Bluetooth headsets promote schizophrenia because it looks like you're talking to yourself." Condemning Photoshop may make for a good media story, but Arnold questions its validity.

In a post here [the *Huffington Post* website] entitled "Photoshop Isn't Evil," Elizabeth Perle wrote that her "knee jerk reaction to hearing this news was a long, exaggerated eye roll." The AMA's statement against Photoshop, she believes is "too little too late," adding it "frankly might make it worse for models, actresses, singers and other performers, for whom the pressures to alter their bodies will only be heightened."

Photographers and artists have their own take on this issue. "We have wonderful tools to create images, new digital cameras and photographic digital printers and powerful tools such as Photoshop and we are expected to do what—nothing? I don't think so," says Jeff Schewe of *Photoshop News*. Some feel the AMA misses the point. Michael Graupman, in "Photoshop on the Chopping Block" writes, "Perhaps it is time for a refresher course for the media and Americans on what Photoshop was created for originally: bringing a subject more into focus, not creating works of fiction." Denouncing Photoshop, many believe, will have little impact on America's distorted view of beauty and that the alteration of images in photography should not be singled out.

A Positive Direction

I disagree. The importance of the AMA's recent policy statement is that it is headed in the right direction. First, let's get the facts straight. Denouncing Photoshop sounds newsworthy, but it was not the focus of the AMA's statement. No one in the medical association—which joins physicians to promote professional and public health issues—talked about completely banning this creative technique from photography. Second, although physicians are studying links between photo distortion in advertising and the rise of eating disorders and other body image pathology, the connection and the solutions have yet to be determined.

Creating an Unrealistic Standard of Beauty

It doesn't take a genius to see that [magazines are] creating a standard of beauty that's far from what the average American reader can attain. Already models weigh about 23 percent less than the average woman. . . . Retouchers today are increasingly asked by advertisers and editors to enlarge eyes, trim ears, fill in hairlines, straighten and whiten teeth and lengthen the already narrow necks, waists and legs of 18-year-old beauties.

Jessica Bennet, Daily Beast, *May 1, 2008.*
www.thedailybeast.com.

The AMA is just beginning to raise public awareness about the impact of image manipulation on childhood development. They want us all to reflect upon the way in which unrealistic imagery may serve as a contributor to adolescent health problems—and to consider creating ground rules for those who present these images to the public. As part of a general move toward overseeing potentially harmful media influences, the AMA suggests that ad agencies work with child and adolescent-focused health organizations to create guidelines for future advertising.

Clearly, these are complicated psychological and sociological issues, in terms of both the underlying causes for the recent explosion of adolescent eating disorders as well as the subtle (and not so subtle) ways the media influence these problems. Just as there have long been questions about the connection between violence on TV and childhood aggression, or between cigarette ads and adolescent smoking, more research is required to know how to move forward on the cultural impact of Photoshop. No doubt, the AMA's recent statement is a step in that direction.

The Policy Options

Perhaps we are headed toward more dramatic policies, like the ones proposed in Europe. Two years ago [2009], French Parliament member Valerie Boyer suggested that all published images that are digitally enhanced—including advertisements, press photos, political campaigns, art photography and product packaging—come with a warning label that reads, "Retouched photograph aimed at changing a person's physical appearance." Failure to do so would lead advertisers to be fined of up to 50 percent of the cost of the publicity campaign in question. With their first lady, Carla Bruni, having been airbrushed hundreds of times as a former supermodel and even President [Nicolas] Sarkozy having his picture Photoshopped in *Paris Match* magazine, this new policy did not go over easily in the French parliament. But, according to Boyer, the proposal was not an attempt to "damage creativity of photographers or publicity campaigns, but to advise the public on whether what they are seeing is real or not."

While America is no stranger to the importance of promoting public health and protecting consumers from false advertising—one of the principal missions of the U.S. Federal Trade Commission since its inception in 1914—it may take many more years before measures like the one in France take off here. Some believe that American photographers, models and the media—who are used to showing off our celebrities as stick-thin and blemish-free—won't go for it. Photoshopping and airbrushing, many believe, are now an inherent part of the beauty industry, as are makeup, lighting and styling. They believe photography is a creative art, a freedom not to be denied for any reason, regardless of its psychological or physical impact. Ultimately, it is hard to know where to draw the line between what requires regulation and what is part of the artistic process.

Supporting Youth Health

Yet we cannot waste any more time arguing about the pros or cons of the AMA's current decision to raise awareness about the health risks of Photoshop. Rather, we need to support the intervention and move it further along. Sure there are debatable issues: Is there enough research to support AMA's concern? Is questioning Photoshop extreme enough? Does it encroach on artistic freedom? Does it deflect from the larger issues—the objectification of women, dehumanization of beauty?

But what is clear is the imperative to relieve our youth of the rampant pressures they feel when it comes to their bodies. We need to question the unrealistic goals set not only by the distorted images in magazines but by those promoted through celebrity makeovers, reality shows, and parents who undergo radical transformations through plastic surgery. I see nothing negative in having medical and psychological experts join with the beauty and advertising industries in an effort to more positively influence young boys and girls. In fact, I applaud them.

Note

1. "DSM-IV" stands for *Diagnostic and Statistical Manual of Mental Disorders*, fourth edition, a publication of the American Psychiatric Association that includes all recognized mental health disorders.

"If you read the studies more closely . . . there's very little mention of linkage [of altered images] to outright, diagnosable eating disorders."

Altered Fashion Magazine Photographs Do Not Cause Eating Disorders

Carrie Arnold

Although viewing distorted fashion magazine images can be harmful, no evidence shows that this practice causes eating disorders, claims Carrie Arnold in the following viewpoint. People often confuse eating disorders such as anorexia and bulimia with disordered eating such as dieting and body dissatisfaction, she maintains. While environmental factors such as media exposure play a role in disordered eating, factors such as genetics, neurobiology, and personality influence the development of eating disorders, Arnold argues. Thus, she reasons, blaming Photoshop is unwarranted. Arnold, a recovering anorexic, is the author of Decoding Anorexia: How Science Offers Hope for Eating Disorders.

As you read, consider the following questions:

1. What was the goal of guidelines that the American Medical Association asked advertising associations to adopt?

2. What did Arnold discover when she searched "eating disorders media" in PubMed?

3. What percentage of American women develop anorexia nervosa or bulimia nervosa, according to the author?

Last week [in June 2011], the American Medical Association [AMA] released a policy statement about Photoshopping models and eating disorder prevention.

The statement:

Advertisers commonly alter photographs to enhance the appearance of models' bodies, and such alterations can contribute to unrealistic expectations of appropriate body image—especially among impressionable children and adolescents. A large body of literature links exposure to media-propagated images of unrealistic body image to eating disorders and other child and adolescent health problems.

The AMA adopted a new policy to encourage advertising associations to work with public and private sector organizations concerned with child and adolescent health to develop guidelines for advertisements, especially those appearing in teen-oriented publications, that would discourage the altering of photographs in a manner that could promote unrealistic expectations of appropriate body image.

"The appearance of advertisements with extremely altered models can create unrealistic expectations of appropriate body image. In one image, a model's waist was slimmed so severely, her head appeared to be wider than her waist," said Dr. McAneny. "We must stop exposing impressionable children and teenagers to advertisements portraying models with body types only attainable with the help of photo editing software."

A Lack of Evidence

And if the AMA had left out the mention of "eating disorders" at the end of the first paragraph, I wouldn't have had anything to say except to nod my head in agreement. Because the alteration of images is appalling and inappropriate and, indeed, harmful. The problem is the link to eating disorders. The AMA said there was a "large body of research" linking media exposure to eating disorders.

So I went looking to see if I could find this large body of research. I went to [journal database] PubMed, and searched for "eating disorders media" and indeed, I pulled up 264 studies on the subject. But if you read the studies more closely, you'll see that there's lots of links between "disordered eating" and "eating pathology" and "body image dissatisfaction" and media exposure, but there's very little mention of linkage to outright, diagnosable eating disorders as spelled out by the DSM-IV.[1] One study did actually say that "media contributes to the development of eating disorders," but when I looked at the studies cited, all I saw were examples that linked media exposure to disordered eating.

A lot of the media coverage of the story has said that Photoshopped images "promote anorexia." I'm not entirely sure I understand what that means. I think I know what they're getting at—that looking at these images makes you more likely to develop anorexia—but there's no actual evidence that this is true (at least, none that I could find). We don't think ads for disinfectant somehow promote OCD [obsessive-compulsive disorder]. We also don't think that those Bluetooth headsets promote schizophrenia because it looks like you're talking to yourself.

A Common Mistake

I think the big difference is that people don't think they know what it's like to have schizophrenia [just] because they've been paranoid at one time or another, or that they've had a rather animated conversation with themselves. But people do think they know what it's like to have an eating disorder because they've dieted and asked their husbands if these jeans make their butts look big.

It's a common mistake, confusing disordered eating and eating disorders. We often think that eating disorders are just extreme diets, when they're not. Many men and women are unhappy with their bodies and are on a diet. People with eating disorders also often express extreme body dysmorphia [bad body image] and restrict their food intake. They do look alike on the outside, but the internal experience is very different. Dr. Sarah Ravin summarizes the difference between disordered eating and eating disorders as follows:

Disordered eating is very widespread in our country, especially among women. I define disordered eating as a persistent pattern of unhealthy or overly rigid eating behavior—chronic dieting, yo-yo dieting, binge-restrict cycles, eliminating essential nutrients such as fat or carbohydrates, obsession with organic or "healthy" eating—coupled with a preoccupation with food, weight, or body shape.

By this definition, I think well over half of the women in America (and many men as well) are disordered eaters.

The way I see it, disordered eating "comes from the outside" whereas eating disorders "come from the inside." What I mean is this: environment plays a huge role in the onset of disordered eating, such that the majority of people who live in our disordered culture (where thinness is overvalued, dieting is the norm, portion sizes are huge, etc.) will develop some degree of disordered eating, regardless of their underlying biology or psychopathology.

In contrast, the development of an eating disorder is influenced very heavily by genetics, neurobiology, individual personality traits, and co-morbid [accompanying] disorders. Environment clearly plays a role in the development of eating disorders, but environment alone is not sufficient to cause them. The majority of American women will develop disordered eating at some point, but less than 1% will fall into anorexia nervosa and 3% into bulimia nervosa.

I think it's great that the AMA is trying to protect children and adolescents from companies that would turn actual women into bobblehead models. . . . Our ideas of what "normal" and "healthy" look like are disorted and it is harmful. On that subject, the research is clear.

Note

1. "DSM-IV" stands for *Diagnostic and Statistical Manual of Mental Disorders*, fourth edition, a publication of the American Psychiatric Association that includes all recognized mental health disorders.

> "The fashion industry's perceived endorsement of thinness at any cost promotes . . . eating disorders."

The Fashion Industry Promotes Eating Disorders

Libby Rodenbough

The fashion industry response to the eating disorder–related deaths of several well known fashion models has been inadequate, maintains Libby Rodenbough in the following viewpoint. The pressure on models to be thin and, in turn, the pressure on others to conform to these unattainable ideals is considerable, she argues. Moreover, Rodenbough reasons, people resort to unhealthy weight-loss techniques such as starvation, self-induced vomiting, and laxatives to try to achieve these unnatural ideals. Unless all elements of the fashion industry work together to make comprehensive changes, people, particularly women and girls, will continue to suffer. Rodenbough, a writer and musician, was at the time of this viewpoint an editorial intern at In These Times, *a progressive newsmagazine.*

As you read, consider the following questions:

1. What did some pro-anorexia and pro-bulimia websites use as "thinspiration," according to Rodenbough?

2. What guidelines did three prominent eating disorder organizations set for the fashion industry, as the author reports?

3. What is the perfect storm of things than can trigger eating disorders, according to Harriet Brown, as cited by Rodenbough?

O n Nov. 17, 2010, anorexia nervosa claimed the life of 28-year-old French model Isabelle Caro, who had spent the last years of her life publicizing the horrors of the disease. Her mother, devastated by grief and guilt, committed suicide several weeks later. In 2007, Caro had appeared in "No Anorexia," an ad campaign by provocative fashion photographer Oliviero Toscani. . . . The images of her naked, grotesquely emaciated body shocked and revolted. The campaign, intended to disassociate unhealthy thinness with connotations of glamour, sparked controversy, in part because some pro-anorexia and -bulimia websites used its ads as "thinspiration" (collections of images or videos of slim to skeletal women used by those suffering from eating disorders for weight-loss motivation). Despite her commitment to heightening awareness of anorexia, Caro could not escape its demons.

Caro's unsettling death recalled a string of fatalities in 2006 and 2007 of fashion models who suffered from eating disorders, which, while highly publicized at the time, had since largely faded from the public's—and the fashion industry's—memory.

On Aug. 2, 2006, moments after stepping off a catwalk in Montevideo, Uruguay, 22-year-old fashion model Luisel Ramos collapsed and died from heart failure believed to have been triggered by self-imposed starvation. Ramos' father reported that she had been subsisting on a diet of lettuce and Diet Coke in anticipation of the show. On Nov. 15, 2006, 21-year-old Brazilian model Ana Carolina Reston died in a São Paulo hospital from generalized infection. Her body had been rendered powerless to fight it by an extended battle with anorexia and bulimia. And on Feb. 13, 2007, Ramos' sister, Eliana, also a model and only 18 years old, was found dead at her grandparents' home, apparently having suffered a heart attack linked to malnutrition.

This rapid succession of casualties provided a wake-up call for the international fashion industry. One detail in particular made it impossible to ignore: All three women, even on the brink of death, were taking home paychecks as working models. The industry responded with regulations varying by country in substance and severity. But the effects of voluntary measures adopted in the United States are unknown, thanks in no small part to the continuing silence of industry leaders and insiders in New York City.

The Industry's Reaction

Within months, the fashion capitals of Madrid, Milan and São Paulo introduced new procedures for their runway shows, such as requiring that participating models pass a doctor's examination or meet a minimum Body Mass Index (BMI) of 18. (BMI is a measure of body fat based on height and weight; the World Health Organization classifies someone with a BMI of less than 18.5 as "underweight.")

Other industry leaders, however, shied away from such specificity. The fashion establishments in London and New York did take steps to address model health, but both opted for conspicuously less explicit regulations. London's British Fashion Council forewent minimum BMI requirements and doctors' assessments, but did produce an action plan of concrete steps to shift the international culture of fashion in a healthier direction. New York's industry leaders, on the other hand, elected only to frame a set of vague guidelines known as the Health Initiative.

The Council of Fashion Designers of America (CFDA), a trade association, issued the initiative in January 2007. It recommends creating a healthy backstage environment at runway

"Hey Pal! Can't You Read?!," cartoon by Max Garcia. www.CartoonStock.com.

shows and referring models with eating disorders to professional help. It also advises that models participating in runway shows should be 16 or older. As in London, missing from the guidelines are minimum BMIs and medical evaluations for models. Also absent: any means to ensure the implementation of the recommendations, which are voluntary.

An Inadequate Response?

Advocacy groups cried foul. Weeks before the release of the Health Initiative, in an unprecedented joint effort, three of the most prominent organizations of their kind in the United States, the Eating Disorders Coalition (EDC), the National Eating Disorders Association (NEDA) and the Academy for Eating Disorders (AED) had formulated their own set of guidelines for the industry.

Their guidelines included a minimum BMI requirement of 18.5 for models over 18 and a graduated system of BMI requirements for younger models. They called for the development of "action steps to identify models in need of intervention." And they proposed an outright ban on airbrushing photos of models to create unrealistically thin images. Furthermore, the AED urged the industry "to institute regular, yearly medical evaluations and developmentally-appropriate medical and psychological screening and assessments for all models."

These nonprofit advocacy groups volunteered their own resources to assist the fashion industry in implementing the above proposals. While they have scant financial resources, these groups do serve to network physicians and other eating disorder experts. Conversely, what the multi-billion dollar fashion industry lacks in medical expertise, it compensates for in revenue. In an e-mail to *In These Times*, Cynthia M. Bulik, director of the University of North Carolina Eating Disorders Program and former president of the AED, wrote: "We have the advocates, we have the brainpower, we have the ability to help build and evaluate programs, but our meager dollars couldn't come close to the depth of their pockets!"

That seemingly fortuitous partnership has yet to become a reality. The CFDA Health Initiative fails to include some of the bolder recommendations of the eating disorder activists. Indeed, preemptively addressing any such criticism, the Initiative reads: "The CFDA Health Initiative is about awareness and education, not policing. Therefore, the committee does not recommend that models get a doctor's physical examination to assess their health or body-mass index to be permitted to work. Eating disorders are emotional disorders that have psychological, behavioral, social, and physical manifestations, of which body weight is only one."

Eating disorders are complex psychiatric disorders, but some experts worry that without concrete screening methods the Health Initiative will be ineffectual. "You can't tell someone's health by the BMI. It is not a perfect indicator. But the American fashion industry did not refuse to use BMI because they don't think it is a good indicator. They basically tried to take the teeth out of any real standards," says Jennifer L. Pozner, founder and executive director of Women in Media and News (WIMN). "Anything that would change the industry and hold them accountable in ways they could not deal with, they rejected."

In These Times asked CDFA if it has taken any specific measures to ensure the effectiveness of the Health Initiative and why it was not requiring a doctor's evaluation to ensure that models are in good physical health. Christine Olsen, CDFA's manager for public relations and special events, refused to answer, saying only, "We do not have a statement to add at this time."

Doctors' evaluations and screening models based on BMI are not foolproof ways to detect eating disorders, but they do have potential benefits. "[The screening methods] can definitely reduce the pressure on models to engage in unhealthy weight control behaviors," says Bulik. "They also help protect the consumers of the fashion industry from constantly being barraged by images of unusually thin women."

High Standards of Beauty

The pressure on models, both female and male, to be thin—and the resultant pressure on girls, boys, women and men to conform to an unattainable ideal—is immense. Because a model's professional success depends almost entirely on appearance, models obsess about their bodies. Yet the physical standards that models feel pressured to meet are unrealistic. A 2002 Centers for Disease

Control report found that the average American woman is 5'4" and weighs 163 pounds; in 2006, it was estimated that the average female fashion model is 5'9" and 110 pounds.

The day-to-day stress of modeling is considerable, chiefly because all but the most famous are easily disposable. If a model doesn't fit into designers' samples, an agency can simply bring in a thinner replacement, and the ousted model has no channel for redress. Dutch model Marvy Rieder, 31, explains, "If you want to work, you have to fit into the clothes. That's not something your agent has to tell you; you come up with it very quickly yourself."

Though modeling has often been cast as a glamorous occupation epitomized by jet-setting socialites like Kate Moss and Gisele Bündchen, very few models are able to achieve such a degree of celebrity or financial security. "You have to realize that modeling is like a pyramid," says Rieder. "The majority of the models are at the bottom of the pyramid. It is a huge layer of really nice, really beautiful girls who cannot make a good living. I compare it to top athletes. They have a period of time when they peak, and then it's over."

Rieder, whose marVie Foundation provides health guidance for models through workshops and trainings, points out that in this survival-of-the-thinnest vocation, runway models in their twenties must compete with 15- and 16-year-old girls. "When I was 15 years old," she says, "I was just thin, and I could eat anything. But every girl . . . develops a female figure. From then on, the pressure increases. You have to stop the natural growth of your body to stay the same."

Rieder's long tenure in the profession has emboldened her to defy the compulsion to sacrifice health for work. She recognizes that her adult body no longer meets the strict expectations for models who walk the glitziest international runways.

Struggling against nature, some models turn to decidedly unnatural weight control methods like laxatives, self-induced vomiting and fasting. When those weight control methods metastasize into a full spectrum eating disorder, models face more serious risks than unemployment. Eating disorders are mental illnesses, and often deadly ones. Anorexia has the highest rate of mortality of any mental illness, at around 20 percent. Eating disorders are more than two times more prevalent in the United States than Alzheimer's disease, although funding for anorexia research is less than one-fiftieth of that for Alzheimer's research.

The causes of eating disorders are not entirely understood, but models are exposed to a conflagration of risk factors. Harriet Brown, a professor at S.I. Newhouse School of Public Communications at Syracuse University, is the author of *Brave Girl Eating*, a memoir about her daughter's struggle with an eating disorder. "You're often triggered by a perfect storm of things, genetics, puberty, hormones and cultural factors among them," she says. "In fact, it's less about triggers and more about aggregation."

Models are often discovered at age 14 or younger, at a time when their bodies—and their feelings about their bodies—are in a state of flux. In 86 percent of reported cases, the onset of an eating disorder occurs before age 20. Compound the susceptibility of youth with a profession that entails continual—and competitive—monitoring of body measurements, and it's no wonder so many models fall victim to eating disorders. "Every model is afraid of being measured," says Rieder. "Every model is afraid of the centimeter."

From Runway to Living Room

That fear is not confined to the world of sample sizes and catwalks. According to *The Journal of Adolescent Health*, 81 percent of American 10-year-olds are afraid of being fat. Of course, very few 10-year-olds attend runway fashion shows. Instead, they—and Americans of all ages—get their "thinspiration" from a variety of media, among them ads for all manner of consumer goods that invariably feature tall, stick-thin models.

The physical ideal established by models on the runway, in ads and on reality TV does not translate directly to eating disorders, but it affects us, both as emotionally vulnerable beings and as consumers. Dr. David B. Herzog, director of the Harris Center for Education and Advocacy in Eating Disorders at the Massachusetts General Hospital, has advised the CFDA on matters of model health. "Most people who look at pictures of high fashion models do not develop eating disorders," he says. "In the people who develop eating disorders, there's a sizeable percentage that have little interest in fashion. It is not at all a direct correlation, but the thin ideal that the industry has had a role in developing . . . has a big impact on how people feel about themselves."

As part of a wider trend, the fashion industry's perceived endorsement of thinness at any cost promotes unhealthy eating practices that, in individuals with existing risk factors, may manifest themselves as anorexia, bulimia, binge eating or other partial- or full-spectrum eating disorders. Some types of disordered eating may progress to obesity; others may lead to severe malnutrition or death.

Where Responsibility Lies

So, who's to blame? The problem can't be fixed until the culprit is determined. Therein lies the roadblock. No one component of the fashion industry seems poised to instigate change.

Modeling agencies are most profitable when they provide the thin models that are popular with designers. Often those designers are gay men whose standard for physical beauty eschews feminine curves. Designers contend that they aren't to blame because all the models are so thin that they are forced to tailor clothing to skeletal frames. Advertisers and manufacturers of a vast spectrum of products profit from existing standards.

Models fear they will be easily replaced by a thinner alternative if they do not conform to the sample size, which is sometimes an American size 00, which is, incomprehensibly, one size less than 0.

The CFDA's tight-lipped response to questions from *In These Times* was echoed by fashion magazine editors, designers and modeling agency representatives. All declined [a] request to comment.

The CFDA has received flak for not ensuring model health with stricter regulations, but it is not properly equipped to resolve the issue on its own. Claire Mysko, former director of the American Anorexia Bulimia Association, puts it this way: "The CFDA is not a union. They don't have the resources to enforce guidelines, and it would take a system to be in place for that to happen." Even if the CFDA were to address model health in a meaningful and specific way, as several organizations devoted to eating disorder awareness already have, it has no regulatory authority to implement such directives. The AED, EDC and other advocacy organizations have offered the CFDA their help, but have received no response from the industry.

Herzog cautions against demonizing the industry. "The question I always get asked is, do I really believe these fashion leaders are serious about change, or do I think I'm being used? I would suggest that they actually are interested in making changes. It's just that it's hard to get all the various parties on board, especially in such a competitive industry," he says. "I do believe, though, that this industry has a responsibility to create healthy images for the public at large."

For the fashion industry to fulfill that responsibility, both to its models and to the public that consumes its products, it will have to undertake comprehensive changes, and in the process go up against entrenched beliefs about the role and purpose of fashion models. Mysko and model Magali Amadei, authors of *Does This Pregnancy Make Me Look Fat?*, suggest that models form a union that could empower them to negotiate the terms of their contracts without fear of losing jobs to an endless stream of ever-thinner—and more desperate—hopefuls.

Direct government regulation is another option. Fashion images do not cause eating disorders or other health conditions, in the same way that cigarette ads do not cause lung cancer nor liquor ads cause alcoholism. Nevertheless, governments have deemed their influence detrimental enough to public health to merit regulation. In the United Kingdom, Britain's Royal College of Psychiatrists suggests that warning symbols be placed on airbrushed images of models alerting viewers to their deceptiveness. And in 2007, Bronx Assemblyman José Rivera proposed legislation that would create a state advisory board to establish standards for the employment of models under the age of 18, in part to help prevent the development of eating disorders.

Until government acts—an unlikely prospect in the laissez-faire United States—America's fashion industry ought to act to quell our dangerous obsession with thinness, or acknowledge its central role in perpetuating it.

> *"The anorexia industry . . . is cynical idolatry masquerading as public concern in order to sell magazines."*

The Media Foster Misplaced Public Concern About Anorexia

Laurie Penny

The media response to the death of fashion models due to complications from anorexia does not reflect concern for these models but a fascination with the disease, claims Laurie Penny in the following viewpoint. The media portray models and teens who struggle with anorexia as vulnerable victims who risk their lives to meet impossible beauty ideals, she argues, and maintains that, in truth, anorexia has deeper root causes. Rather than blame extreme beauty ideals, women and girls must learn that they deserve to eat and to be imperfect and powerful, Penny concludes. Penny writes on pop culture and politics from a feminist perspective for the New Statesman, *a British newsmagazine.*

As you read, consider the following questions:

1. What does Penny claim Isabelle Caro won upon becoming the "face" of anorexia?

2. Who does the author claim may be deliberately ignored by the expansion of the anorexia industry?
3. According to the author, why is it inevitable that the image of the anorexic should fascinate us?

A nother day, another dainty dead girl. The premature passing of the French model Isabelle Caro from complications due to anorexia nervosa is as tragic as it is unsurprising. Caro, 28, was the face of the world-famous Nolita campaign, a poster project designed to show dieting teenagers the horrific effects of anorexia on the body.

After the campaign, Caro briefly became the darling of the shock press. Modelling contracts poured in, as did talk-show appearances and a book deal for her short, painful autobiography, *The Little Girl Who Didn't Want to Get Fat*. Being the "face" of anorexia won Caro fame, praise and attention—everything she had ever craved. Everything apart from life and health.

A Self-Defeating Rebellion

When Naomi Wolf wrote *The Beauty Myth* in 1990, she observed that the rising epidemic of serious eating disorders, which affect an estimated 3 per cent of young women in the developed world, was passing under the radar of the global press. Twenty years later, anorexia has become a global obsession.

One can hardly open a newspaper without reading another gushing interview with a teenager battling the disease, or turn on the television without seeing another gruesome documentary blithely illustrated with pictures of pouting, half-naked waifs, featured just before speculation over what [singer and fashion designer] Victoria Beckham didn't have for breakfast. The press might not admit it but anorexia is in fashion.

The anorexia industry, for which poor Caro was briefly the mascot, is cynical idolatry masquerading as public concern in order to sell magazines. The anorexic has become the famished saint of late-capitalist femininity: beautiful, vulnerable and pre-pared to risk everything to conform to society's standards. Hers is a self-defeating rebellion against the sexist surveillance of pa-triarchal culture.

"Thinspiration" and Its Appeal

Over two decades of gory "awareness raising", real public un-derstanding of eating disorders has barely improved. Nor have treatment standards—more than 50 per cent of anorexics never recover. The poster campaign in which Caro was involved back-fired spectacularly because it was based on the assumption that anorexic women starve themselves to look more "beautiful", rather than because of any deeper trauma.

Naked pictures of her still appear on "pro-anorexia" web-sites, which are designed to give "thinspiration" to self-starvers. As the anorexia industry expands, people with less glamorous but equally destructive disorders such as bulimia nervosa and compulsive overeating are deliberately ignored—as are the many sufferers who happen to be male, poor, non-white or simply unphotogenic.

As a former anorexia sufferer, I have been approached to write the woeful story of my teenage illness, not once, but sev-eral times. I refused because the nation's bookstores are already overflowing with sob stories stuffed with grisly details of vomit-ing techniques. When I was sick, I used to read those books for weight-loss tips.

In a society where anxiety about consumption has become the defining collective neurosis, it is, perhaps, inevitable that the image of the anorexic should fascinate us. We are perplexed by the self-starver's ability to transcend the needs of the flesh and, at the same time, compelled by it. More importantly, the fashion for anorexia taps into an increasingly popular loathing for female flesh—and fear of female flesh is fear of female power.

One thing is for sure: the anorexia industry has little to do with concern for women's welfare. If we truly want to protect young women from the siren song of self-starvation, it's not enough to persuade them that "skinny isn't beautiful"—we must communicate the conviction that all women deserve to take up space, to nourish ourselves, and to be large and imperfect and unashamedly powerful.

Periodical and Internet Sources Bibliography

The following articles have been selected to supplement the diverse views presented in this chapter.

Julie M. Albright

"Impossible Bodies: TV Viewing Habits, Body Image, and Plastic Surgery Attitudes Among College Students in Los Angeles and Buffalo, New York," *Configurations*, Spring 2007.

Hilary Alexander

"Size Zero: The Blame Couture," *Daily Telegraph*, September 9, 2007.

Jessica Bennett

"Picture Perfect," *Daily Beast*, May 1, 2008. www.thedailybeast .com.

Jennifer Cognard-Black

"Extreme Makeover: Feminist Edition," *Ms.*, Summer 2007.

Lucy Danziger

"Pictures That Please Us," *Lucy's Blog*, August 10, 2009. www.self .com.

Alene Dawson

"Looks; Just the Way You Are; Don't Fall Victim to Impossible Standards of Beauty, Experts Say. Embrace Your Uniqueness," *Los Angeles Times*, January 8, 2012.

Shaun Dreisbach

"Retouching: How Much Is Too Much?," *Glamour*, February 2012.

Jennifer D. Gaertner

"Mainstream Standards of Beauty," *Evangelical Outpost*, April 2010. www.evanelicaloutpost.com.

Beth Hale

"Fashion Fails to Act over the Size Zero Freak Show," *Daily Mail*, January 26, 2007.

Virginia Heffernan

"The Pixelated Face," *New York Times Magazine*, June 27, 2010.

Mary Sanchez

"For Healthier Female Body Images, Let's Drop Photoshop," *Kansas City Star*, December 5, 2011.

For Further Discussion

Chapter 1

1. Glenn Wilson claims that principles of evolutionary biology determine standards of beauty. Michal Brichacek and Robert Moreland assert that standards of facial beauty are universal while standards of body beauty vary among cultures. While Wilson agrees that facial beauty standards do appear to be universal, how do the authors differ in how they define cultural influences? In your opinion, does this make one viewpoint more persuasive than the other? Why or why not?

2. Deborah L. Rhode believes that the media influence standards of beauty. Susie Orbach argues that the drive to profit from women's insecurities has led to increasingly unachievable beauty standards. Identify the types of evidence each author uses to support her argument. Which type of evidence do you find more persuasive? Explain.

3. How do the affiliations of the authors in this chapter influence their rhetoric? What rhetorical strategy do you find most persuasive? Explain.

Chapter 2

1. Natasha Walter argues that because of society's emphasis on beauty, women are valued more for their appearance than their work. Raina Kelley does not disagree. However, she claims that women should focus instead on the many opportunities available to them. What evidence does each author provide to support her claim? Does this evidence make one viewpoint more persuasive? Explain.

2. Deborah L. Rhode claims that discrimination against unattractive people in the workplace is a serious problem. Mary Elizabeth Williams does not dispute that in some cases discrimination against unattractive people is unfair.

Nevertheless, she maintains, in some cases businesses require attractive employees to inspire sales. What rhetorical strategy does each author use to express her views? Which do you find more persuasive? Explain.

3. What commonalities do you find in the rhetoric on both sides of the debate concerning the impact of beauty ideals on society in this chapter?

4. Which societal impacts do you think have the greatest influence? To what extent, if any, is your decision based on your understanding of how beauty ideals are established? Explain.

Chapter 3

1. Amy Alkon maintains that it is important to strive for beauty as an attractive appearance helps women get jobs and mates. Shari Graydon argues, on the other hand, that the pursuit of beauty can be dangerous for girls and women. Note the authors' affiliations. How do their affiliations influence their rhetoric? Which rhetorical strategy do you find more persuasive? Explain.

2. *Biotech Week*'s viewpoint reports on a type of plastic surgery that increases patient satisfaction and self-esteem. Alexander Edmonds, on the other hand, writes that cosmetic surgery is not necessary to improve health and has many risks that do not outweigh the benefits. Edmonds' viewpoint was published in a general-interest newspaper and *Biotech Week* is a magazine for the biotechnology and pharmaceutical industries. How do the two viewpoints differ in their approaches? Does the original audience influence each viewpoint's rhetoric? Which do you find most persuasive? Explain using examples from each viewpoint.

3. What commonalities among the evidence and rhetoric can you find in the viewpoints on both sides of the debate in this chapter? What impact do these strategies have on the viewpoints' persuasiveness? Explain.

Chapter 4

1. How are the authors' differing views on the role of the fashion and beauty industries reflected in their views on the effects of these industries? What do the viewpoints on both sides of these debates have in common and how do they differ?

2. Vivian Diller argues that magazine photos altered by technology that creates unrealistic images of beauty pose a threat to teens. Carrie Arnold does not dispute that unrealistic images may impact teens but claims there is no evidence that these images lead to eating disorders and thus blaming these technologies is misplaced. What evidence does each author provide to support her view? Which evidence do you find more persuasive? Why?

3. Libby Rodenbough maintains that the fashion industry is not doing enough to reduce the pressure on models to be thin and, in turn, the pressure on those who strive to achieve these unattainable ideals. Laurie Penny asserts that the concern over fashion industry models reveals more about the public's unnatural obsession with anorexia than a concern for fashion models. How do the rhetorical strategies of these two authors differ? Which do you find more persuasive? Explain.

4. Several authors in this and previous chapters argue that media literacy is necessary to counter the impact of unrealistic beauty ideals perpetuated by entertainment media and the beauty and fashion industries. Others suggest that these industries should meet guidelines that protect women and girls from their influence. Still others argue that broader social concerns are the source of poor body image among women and girls. How do the authors' recommended solutions to the problem characterize their views on the culture of beauty? Which solution do you think will best address these concerns? Explain.

Organizations to Contact

The editors have compiled the following list of organizations concerned with the issues debated in this book. The descriptions are derived from materials provided by the organizations. All have publications or information available for interested readers. The list was compiled on the date of publication of the present volume; names, addresses, phone and fax numbers, and e-mail and Internet addresses may change. Be aware that many organizations take several weeks or longer to respond to inquiries, so allow as much time as possible.

About-Face
PO Box 77665
San Francisco, CA 94107
(415) 839-6779
website: www.about-face.org

About-Face believes that women and girls are inundated with messages that they must be tall, blonde, tan, and sexually available. These messages, the organization reasons, contribute to a host of ills, from low self-esteem to eating disorders, that limit women's ability to achieve their full potential. Thus, About-Face promotes self-esteem in girls and women through workshops and activism. On its website About-Face links users to fact sheets on body image, media, eating disorders, and cosmetic surgery compiled by organization experts with links to the studies from which the facts were compiled.

American Psychological Association (APA)
750 First Street NE
Washington, DC 20002-4242
(202) 336-5500; toll-free: (800) 374-2721
website: www.apa.org

Based in Washington, DC, APA is a scientific and professional organization that represents psychology in the United States. With 150,000 members, APA is the largest association of psychologists worldwide. It publishes articles and reports on beauty, cosmetic surgery, and other related topics in its numerous journals as well as books, including *Body Image, Eating Disorders, and Obesity in Youth* and *Self-Objectification in Women*. Many of the organization's articles are available on its website.

Academy for Eating Disorders (AED)
111 Deer Lake Road, Suite 100
Deerfield, IL 60015
(847) 498-4274 • fax: (847) 480-9282
e-mail: info@aedweb.org
website: www.aedweb.org

AED is an international organization for eating disorder treatment, research, and education. It provides cutting-edge professional training and education; inspires new developments in eating disorders research, prevention, and clinical treatments; and is the international source for state-of-the-art information in the field of eating disorders. The AED believes that the beauty and fashion industries should promote a healthy body image and address eating disorders within the modeling profession.

American Society of Plastic Surgeons (ASPS)
444 E. Algonquin Road
Arlington Heights, IL 60005
(847) 228-9900
website: www.plasticsurgery.org

ASPS is the largest plastic surgery specialty organization in the world. Established in 1931, the society offers patients and consumers information on cosmetic and reconstructive surgery procedures, an online database of plastic surgery statistics, and technology briefs on the latest developments and advances in the field.

Color Foundation
e-mail: info@colorfoundation.org
website: www.colorfoundation.org

Color Foundation, an independent international organization, furthers activities on biological and social aspects of skin color to improve relations between people worldwide. The organization focuses on issues such as the evolution of skin color and the history of free or forced migration of people in order to understand the past and present attitude toward skin color. Information on skin color can be found on Color Foundation's website and blog.

Common Sense Media
650 Townsend Street, Suite 375
San Francisco, CA 94103
(415) 863-0600 • fax: (415) 863-0601
website: www.commonsensemedia.org

Common Sense Media believes that America's children spend more time with media and digital activities than they do with their families or in school, which profoundly impacts their social, emotional, and physical development. Thus, the organization provides trustworthy information and tools, as well as an independent forum, so that families can have a choice and a voice about the media their children consume. On its website Common Sense provides research on media use by children and expert advice and commentary such as "The Ugly Truth Behind Pretty Pictures" and "How TV Can Save Your Daughter (Sort of)."

Council of Fashion Designers of America (CFDA)
65 Bleecker Street, Floor 11
New York, NY 10012
e-mail: info@cdfa.com
website: www.cfda.com

The CFDA is a not-for-profit trade association of more than 350 of America's foremost fashion and accessory designers. Founded in 1962, the CFDA continues to advance the status of fashion design as a branch of American art and culture, to raise its artistic and professional standards, to define a code of ethical practices of mutual benefit in public and trade relations, and to promote appreciation of the fashion arts through leadership in quality and aesthetic discernment. CFDA's Annual Report, available on its website, provides an overview of current American fashion trends. Also available on its website is information on the CDFA Health Initiative, which supports model health, diversity, and the message that Health is Beauty.

Environmental Working Group (EWG)
1436 U Street NW, Suite 100
Washington, DC 20009
(202) 667-6982
website: www.ewg.org

EWG is a nonprofit organization whose mission is to use the power of public information to protect public health and the environment. EWG's Skin Deep link includes a searchable safety guide database of more than fifty thousand cosmetics and personal care products. The Skin Deep link also publishes news and research on cosmetics and personal care products, including "Eight Myths About Cosmetics Safety."

Food and Drug Administration (FDA)
10903 New Hampshire Ave.
Silver Spring, MD 20993
(888) 463-6332
website: www.fda.gov

The FDA is an agency within the US Department of Health and Human Services and one of the nation's oldest consumer protection agencies. Its mission is to promote and protect the public health by helping safe and effective products reach the market; to monitor products for continued safety after they are in use; and to help the public get the accurate, science-based information needed to improve health. The FDA provides information on the ingredients and labeling of cosmetics and personal care products within its "Cosmetics" link, including a cosmetics Q & A fact sheet, information on how the FDA evaluates cosmetics, and recent recalls and alerts.

National Women's Health Network (NWHN)
1413 K Street NW, 4th Floor
Washington, DC 20005
(202) 682-2640 • fax: (202) 682-2648
e-mail: nwhn@nwhn.org
website: http://nwhn.org

Founded in 1975, the goal of NWHN is to give women a greater voice within the health-care system. The network improves the health of all women by developing and promoting a critical analysis of health issues in order to affect policy and support consumer decision making. NWHN also monitors the actions of federal regulatory and funding agencies, industry, and the health professions; identifies and exposes abuses; and catalyzes grassroots action. On its website NWHN provides access to articles on body image and cosmetic surgery, including "Cosmetic Mutilation? Shameless Self-Confidence!," "Bridalplasty—the Only Show Where the 'Winner' Gets Cut," "Plus-Size Modeling Is a Misstep in the Right Direction," and "The Madwoman in the Mirror."

Love Your Body Campaign, National Organization for Women (NOW)
PO Box 1848
Merrifield, VA 22116-9899
(202) 628-8669
website: http://loveyourbody.nowfoundation.org

NOW developed the Love Your Body campaign to challenge the message that a woman's value is best measured through her willingness and ability to embody current beauty standards. NOW believes that routine objectification and sexualization of women in the media and other cultural institutions can lead to anxiety, shame, self-disgust, undermined confidence, and discomfort with one's own body. Thus, the beauty template women are expected to follow is extremely narrow, unrealistic, and frequently hazardous to their health. The Love Your Body campaign helps women spread the word about the hazards of the media's narrow beauty ideals and sexualization of women and girls. On the Love Your Body website, NOW publishes fact sheets and statistics on body image, eating disorders, cosmetics, and cosmetic surgery. The website also provides links to the video presentation "Sex, Stereotypes and Beauty: The ABCs and Ds of Commercial Images of Women."

Personal Care Products Council (PCPC)
1101 Seventeenth Street NW, Suite 300
Washington, DC 20036-4702
(202) 331-1770 • fax: (202) 331-1969
website: www.personalcarecouncil.org

PCPC (formerly the Cosmetic, Toiletry and Fragrance Association) is a national trade association for the cosmetic and personal care products industry and represents the most innovative names in beauty today. For more than six hundred member companies, the council is the voice on scientific, legal, regulatory, legislative, and international issues for the personal care product industry. PCPC also sponsors a website for consumers, www.cosmeticsinfo.org, which contains information about the safety, testing, and regulation of cosmetics and personal care products and their ingredients.

Bibliography of Books

Sue Abel, Marjan deBruin, and Anita Nowak, eds.	*Women, Advertising and Representation: Beyond Familiar Paradigms.* Cresskill, NJ: Hampton, 2010.
Eric J. Bailey	*Black America, Body Beautiful: How the African American Image Is Changing Fashion, Fitness, and Other Industries.* Westport, CT: Praeger, 2008.
Bonnie Berry	*Beauty Bias: Discrimination and Social Power.* Westport, CT: Praeger, 2007.
Paula Black	*Beauty Industry: Gender, Culture, Pleasure.* New York: Routledge, 2004.
Maxine Leeds Craig	*Ain't I a Beauty Queen? Black Women, Beauty, and the Politics of Race.* New York: Oxford University Press, 2002.
Nancy Etcoff	*Survival of the Prettiest: The Science of Beauty.* New York: Anchor, 2000.
Emily Fox-Kales	*Body Shots: Hollywood and the Culture of Eating Disorders.* Albany, NY: State University of New York Press, 2011.
Evelyn Nakano Glenn	*Shades of Difference: Why Skin Color Matters.* Stanford, CA: Stanford University Press, 2009.

Shari Graydon

In Your Face: The Culture of Beauty and You. Toronto: Annick, 2004.

Daniel S. Hamermesh

Beauty Pays: Why Attractive People Are More Successful. Princeton, NJ: Princeton University Press, 2011.

Stephen P. Hinshaw

The Triple Bind: Saving Our Teenage Girls from Today's Pressures. New York: Ballantine, 2009.

Geoffrey Jones

Beauty Imagined: A History of the Global Beauty Industry. Oxford, England: Oxford University Press, 2010.

Stacy Malkan

Not Just a Pretty Face: The Ugly Side of the Beauty Industry. Gabriola Island, BC: New Society, 2007.

James Northrop

Reflecting on Cosmetic Surgery: Body Image, Shame and Narcissism. New York: Routledge, 2012.

Siobhan O'Connor and Alexandra Spunt

No More Dirty Looks: The Truth About Your Beauty Products—and the Ultimate Guide to Safe and Clean Cosmetics. Cambridge, MA: Da Capo, 2010.

Peggy Orenstein

Cinderella Ate My Daughter: Dispatches from the Front Lines of the New Girlie-Girl Culture. New York: HarperCollins, 2011.

Rhian Parker

Women, Doctors and Cosmetic Surgery: Negotiating the 'Normal' Body. New York: Palgrave Macmillan, 2010.

Kathy Peiss	*Hope in a Jar: The Making of America's Beauty Culture.* Philadelphia: University of Pennsylvania Press, 2011.
Jayne Raisborough	*Lifestyle Media and the Formation of the Self.* New York: Palgrave Macmillan, 2011.
Viren Swami and Adrian Furham, eds.	*The Body Beautiful: Evolutionary and Sociocultural Perspectives.* New York: Palgrave Macmillan, 2007.
Shirley Anne Tate	*Black Beauty: Aesthetics, Stylization, Politics.* Burlington, VT: Ashgate, 2009.
Mark Tungate	*Branded Beauty: How Marketing Changed the Way We Look.* Philadelphia: Kogan Page, 2011.
Brenda Weber	*Makeover TV: Selfhood, Citizenship, and Celebrity.* Durham, NC: Duke Univesrity Press, 2009.
Bernadette Wegenstein	*The Cosmetic Gaze: Body Modification and the Construction of Beauty.* Cambridge, MA: MIT Press, 2012.
Ruth Winter	*A Consumer's Dictionary of Cosmetic Ingredients.* New York: Three Rivers, 2009.
Naomi Wolf	*The Beauty Myth: How Images of Beauty Are Used Against Women.* New York: Morrow, 1991. Reprint, New York: HarperPerennial, 2002.

Index